A Fire in My Lens

A Fire in My Lens

An Insider's Look at New Orleans

Armand "Sheik" Richardson

PELICAN PUBLISHING COMPANY
Gretna 2018

ISBN: 9781455624065
Ebook ISBN: 9781455624072

Front-jacket photograph: Each year since 1872, many Mardi Gras night parades are lit up by kerosene-fueled torches known to every New Orleanian as flambeaux. The first were made by James Richardson, so I have always felt a very special connection to them. Historical accounts say that, at one time, as many as 700 would light up a parade. I can recall standing on St. Charles Avenue two blocks from the "Circle" in the 1950s and seeing the sky glow orange when they were lit up on either Napoleon or Jackson Avenue at Tchoupitoulas. This picture was taken at the start of the Orpheus parade, at Napoleon and the river, at sunset on March 3, 2014. It can take many years of waiting for that tiny window of opportunity when all the elements line up perfectly to get a shot like this.

Printed in Malaysia

Published by Pelican Publishing Company, Inc.
1000 Burmaster Street, Gretna, Louisiana 70053
www.pelicanpub.com

The year was 1972, and things were not going well. On a weekly basis, Vietnam was still claiming the lives of many I had either grown up with, gone to school with, or served with in the U.S. Marine Corps or U.S. Navy. There was no end in sight. It was very much like today, only now the KIAs are the children of those I just mentioned. Robert Solerzano Fornier Cortez was the very first from Louisiana to die in Vietnam. He sat next to me in high school and we both joined the Marines in 1964. Bobby was not an American citizen; his father was a diplomat from Nicaragua. But in the infinite lust for young men to send into an old man's war for profit, Bobby was eligible for the draft after losing his deferment because, in 1964, an English professor at UNO decided that "a Hispanic was not worthy of a passing grade." Bobby decided that if he was going to go, he wanted to serve with the best, as did I. So we both went in and signed our names, he as a regular and me as an aviation officer candidate. Bobby served with distinction and had only three days left on his thirteen-month tour when a night mission was called. The squad drew straws and Bobby was not supposed to go. He took the place of another Marine who had a family, and out there somewhere near Chu Lai, he was killed by enemy fire. We had already planned his welcome-home party; decorations, a cake, all were ready. And then the phone call came. "Bobby is dead." At that moment I knew what has been proven ever since. "War for profit" is not spreading democracy or peace.

It was a cold, windy day when I went out behind Fitzgerald's at West End with a Leica camera, an Angenieux zoom lens, and only one roll of film. I wanted to shoot a picture that would forever remind me of Bobby and what he did that night. So I stood there for hours that seemed like years, watching a sun slowly descend into a glowing bronze. I knew exactly what I wanted, a bird flying into the sun. I had only $2.87 in my pocket. Back then you could get a burger for that, or you could get one roll of 5247 movie film processed and get both slides and negatives returned. When the moment came, it was somewhere around 1/2000th of a second. But there it was. I pressed the shutter and could only hope that I had caught it just right. So here it is, all these years later, and it still feels as if I am standing there in dress blues listening to the mournful sound of that bugle. Young men are still being wasted so that old cowardly men and women we now know as "chicken hawks" can thump their chests and feel good about waving the flag, when they never had the courage to do what Bobby did and never will. The name of the picture says more than all these words ever can: "Semper Fi, *Bobby Cortez,* Semper Fi."

Contents

INTRODUCTION

I was fortunate to have been born in New Orleans, a city known the world over as the "Paris of America" during its Golden Age. Little did I know how much that city and its traditions would color the entirety of my life. It's a magical story, one tinted with all the hues of sound, sights, and smells of the Crescent City. Looking back over these many years, I can see why people are drawn here, almost as if by magnetism, and why so many come back or even wind up living here for the rest of their lives. Those were the times when no one born in New Orleans ever wanted to leave, and generations of families often lived next to one another on the same block all of their lives.

One of the very first things I remember seeing was the amazing process of a black and white image suddenly appearing on a blank piece of photo paper immersed in developer under a yellow light. I had to be only one or two years old, because my father had to hold me over the tray so I could see. The image was of my deceased uncle Sheik, for whom I am named. I got his real name, his "nickname," his silver Conn trumpet, and the original photograph that hangs in my hall today. I think my connection with that image stimulated my interest in photography, which has lasted a lifetime.

I grew up surrounded by cameras and learned to crawl on a darkroom floor. So I guess one could say that I was predestined to devote so much of my life to the science and art of imagery. Ironically, when I was a senior in high school, my father offered me all of his equipment and said, "Why don't you start a business?" My answer was: "I want to be an engineer. I won't ever do that, so let's just sell it all." Photography was the last thing on my mind. It was not until 1971 that I first looked through the viewfinder of a Pentax SP 500 and really liked what the world looked like through that 50mm lens. So one day, I took my entire check from working at Model Cities and bought a Pentax camera. On my very first outing with it, I was in City Park near the Delgado Museum, today's New Orleans Museum of Art. It was freezing cold and raining, and the prospect of going into the then-free museum was very inviting indeed. When I got inside there was this huge crowd, and as everyone started moving towards the small auditorium, I wound up sitting in the last row, number twenty-eight, and wondering what everyone was so excited about. The lights went down and a voice said, "Welcome to the Harvey Hysell celebration of the birthday of Edgar Degas."

Little did I know that once again, fate was taking over as the light above the small stage ever so dimly lit up the center of the stage. A vision of something I had never seen before manifested, much as the image of my namesake uncle did on that piece of photographic paper some twenty-five years earlier. Instinctively, I raised my new camera, set the ASA on 1600 for Tri X film, and took a light reading. It registered 1.5 seconds at 2.8, which is an impossible shot handheld. But being inspired enough by what I saw on the stage, I looked through the viewfinder, focused, and pushed the shutter button. As the dancers on the stage created various Degas scenes, I kept shooting, even though at times they were moving so fast it seemed like nothing but a vapor against a black sky. I had no idea whether or not I was getting anything, but I sure did like what I saw inside that frame. I could not wait to get home to develop the film. I had read almost every photography book at the city's main library and had heard of "push processing," so I decided to do exactly that. In my First Street apartment, I had only space heaters and very little hot water, so I decided that if 68 degrees Fahrenheit was good, 100 degrees Fahrenheit was better. I developed that film for twenty-five minutes instead of eight and had no idea what was going to register on it. After "stopping" development with nearly ice water that was coming out of my faucet, I decided to pull out the film and see if anything was on it. To my complete disappointment, the film was almost perfectly clear, virtually nothing on it. So I threw it on the floor and figured it was no great loss anyway. For the next six weeks, I went about experimenting with pushing film and learning how to get better results.

One night, I was trying to demonstrate to an acquaintance (whose name I long ago forgot) how this "photo thing" just might be something I would like to do. I will never know why, but I reached down to the floor below the enlarger, pulled up those Degas tribute negatives, and put one strip into the negative carrier. I knew that, with a very thin negative, exposure time would be short, so I went with F 16 at one-tenth of a second. I was using Grade 5 paper, which normally requires more light than the usual Grade 2. This generally would yield a blank sheet of paper in development, but going on instinct alone, I threw the exposed paper into the developer and, in the customary sixty seconds, an image started to appear. I was absolutely amazed to see what to me looked very much like the same effect I had seen in Robert Capa's picture of Trotsky. I pulled the 11x14 print out of the fixer and turned to show it to my associate, who had now become critical of my idea, but she had already walked out the door, saying, "Nothing will ever come of this. You are wasting your life." Two things happened in that instant. I realized I should never listen to a critic, and what I was seeing on that paper was far beyond anything I had ever hoped I could do with a camera. As she closed the door behind her, another was opening to the entire world, even if I did not know it yet. Thirty-seven years later, when I attended a seminar by Richard Sexton and saw the negative for Ansel Adams' masterpiece "Moonrise," I understood his axiom, "The negative is the musical score; the print is the performance." Richard revealed that the negative was so badly underexposed that it took 200 tries to get the "perfect" print.

As anyone who starts out with a camera will do, I started showing my pictures to a few people to see if they had any merit or if I was just imagining that they were "good."

I showed the ballet print to an artist from Paris, another from New Orleans with a master's degree in art from Louisiana State University, and several co-workers at City Hall, and all of them encouraged me to keep going. A few of them even suggested I put that picture into the *City Hall Talk Magazine* contest. I submitted it just to silence their insistence and to my incredible surprise, it came in third. Not long after, I got a call from the Delgado Museum, and they wanted to see me about these Degas pictures I had done in their building. They said they wanted to buy them and put them on display, and I was floored. When I asked where they would hang them, they said alongside the other pictures in the museum's collection. By then I knew what an Ansel Adams "Moonrise" or a Capa "Trotsky" was, and I really could not believe what I was hearing. Still, they insisted that they wanted to buy the pictures, and when I asked how much the museum would pay, I was told two dollars each. Today that series of dance pictures is on my wall and not in the hands of anyone else.

People told me that I should have won the *City Hall Talk Magazine* contest, but I was not interested in competitions. I just liked making the dance pictures and giving them to people. A few people started saying, "You must do more of this; you must meet Lelia." Who is Lelia? I had no idea, but everyone, including Valerie Smith, a former student of Lelia's and a principal dancer with Ballet Russe de Monte Carlo, was telling me to meet her. So, I went over to the Haller Studio on Harrison Avenue and met Bobbe Haller, who was the daughter of Lelia Haller, the most famous ballerina to ever come from New Orleans. Bobbe looked at the pictures and, like everyone else, told me, "You have to meet Lelia." I found out later that

Ms. Haller was the first New Orleanian to become a principal dancer with the Paris Opera Ballet.

So there she was, all four feet ten inches of pure George Patton in ballet shoes! I was instantly aware that I was in the presence of someone who had a charisma far beyond anyone I had met before. She looked at the pictures and said, “You should do this. Now take off your shoes and let me see your feet.” What? At age twenty-eight, with surgeries on both feet that removed the nerves destroyed during Marine boot camp, I told Ms. Lelia, “I don’t think I can ever do this because I have no feeling in my feet.”

About this time, yet another avenue opened up, one deeply rooted in the New Orleans traditional jazz that I had heard and played since I was able to hold a trumpet. I learned to read music and was exposed to virtually every kind of music, but New Orleans jazz was what lit up my life. From the earliest age I had heard Tony Almerico on the radio and played along as best I could with the Original Assuntos’ Dukes of Dixieland LP records. My father had brought me to the Horace Heidt radio show at the Municipal Auditorium, where the Dukes played their very first performance, and I have to admit that was a life-changing moment for me. Sometimes on a Saturday morning we went to see the Dawnbusters radio program broadcast from the Roosevelt Hotel. That show was broadcast six days a week from 6:15 until 9:00 A.M. live on WWL radio. WWL was a clear-channel station that could be heard all over the world, so we could listen to the show even when we were out of town. The concept of the broadcast was to provide music, singing, and humor to “wake New Orleans up” every morning. One of the opening lines of the original song was, “Hey, Walter! It’s 6:15!” At that show, I met and sat with Al Hirt and got to know what truly great trumpet playing was like.

When we would go to pick up my mother from the dayshift at Hotel Dieu Hospital, we would often stop at Esplanade and Claiborne to watch and listen to the funeral street music that was beyond anything I had ever heard. My father knew Frog Joseph (who played trombone with Joe Turner, Dave Bartholomew, Ray Charles, Louis Cottrell, and several of the other jazz greats), possibly from when my father had played saxophone and went to jam sessions and parades when he was younger. As a result I got to meet, know, and eventually play with many of them after the curse of segregation ended. When I met Gregg Stafford at one of the concerts and second lines I frequently went to, the jazz door opened wide, and I spent the next forty-four years playing, photographing, and being totally immersed in the world of jazz.

It was not until the 1980s that I discovered I have other links to the traditions of New Orleans. I knew that my grandfather had been king of the Krewe of Druids and their national chairman in 1930, but I did not know at the time that James Richardson had made the first flambeau torches in 1872. As I dug deeper, I also learned that in December 1814 and January 1815, at least three of my ancestors (George, William, and James Richardson) had fought at the Battle of New Orleans and helped defeat the British at Chalmette.

All of these influences and experiences gave me an insight into a New Orleans that tourists and even many locals never know. Imagine walking down the street with greats such as Jack Willis (Ray Charles’ first trumpet for nineteen years), Lawrence Trotter (Papa Celestin’s drummer), Danny Barker (legendary singer, guitarist, and banjo player who was in Louis Armstrong’s band), Milton Batiste (of the Olympia Brass Band), and Henry Dudley (grand marshal of the Onward, Young Tuxedo, and other bands) just a block from your grandfather’s sheet-metal shop on Kentucky Street in the Ninth Ward, playing “Gettysburg March,” or marching with Charles Barbarin, playing the song his uncle wrote, “Bourbon Street Parade.” How about sitting in Danny Barker’s living room eating “Blue Lu’s” red beans and rice, or playing “Just a Moment of Your Time” with Roland (Leblanc) Stone in a garage in Gentilly? Then of course there is marching with the Krewe of Dreux, Tucks, and the Gentilly Brass Band.

Through photography, I gained life experiences as well as the wisdom of everyone I got to know. Danny Barker told me that he went with Louis Armstrong on his first trip to Chicago and then on to New York. When they got to New York, he said, they went to the union hall and Louis was dressed in his New Orleans finest: a yellow box-back coat, red tie, brown pants, and yam-colored shoes with white socks. He only had an old beat-up trumpet case to carry his horn into the crowded hall. As snickers and jeers were being exchanged around the room by those assembled there, Louis took out his horn and let loose with a "warmup" that must have blown the roof off the building. The next day when they returned to see if there were any jobs lined up for them, everyone in the room was wearing a yellow coat, red tie, brown pants, and yam-colored shoes. Having heard Satchmo play just one time live in the sixties when he came to the Loyola Field House, I can understand why they all went out and got those loud clothes!

Herman Sherman, leader of the Young Tuxedo Jazz Band, was an endless source of stories and humor. When the *Jazz Begins* LP was made in the fifties, Sherman was the "baby" of the band. One time he called me up and said, "Tomorrow, we got a big jazz funeral out on Causeway Boulevard in between Airline and Jefferson Highway. Meet us there at 10:00 A.M. sharp." I gathered up my two cameras, a Leica M5 and a Leica SL with the Angenieux zoom lens, pointed the trusty Ghia convertible out west, and got there about 9:30. Sherman had gathered up a very large band that day—must have been fifteen or more—and everyone was really up for the "gig." A couple of video crews showed up from the local TV news stations, along with reporters from the newspapers, so word must have gotten around somehow. It was cold and windy but everyone was still looking forward to playing. There weren't even the paparazzi that normally showed up for something like this, so it seemed like an "insider" invitation. We waited and waited at the bar where we were supposed to start, and after about forty-five minutes someone arrived and said, "There is no funeral today." Everyone had a good laugh and we realized that somebody had played a joke on Herman. He was a philosophical man, though, and he said, "From now on we gonna make sure we got someone dead to play for."

In addition to photographing ballet dancers, jazz greats, and second-liners while occasionally dodging bullets in the rough streets, I have used forensic photography to assist in cases where injured parties are at the mercy of insurance companies, adjusters, and giant corporations motivated only by the "bottom line." A dead victim is worth less than a live one. When I can help someone like that get justice and have a second chance at life, it justifies all the difficulties and nightmares that doing this type of photography can entail. In *Toups vs. Sears Roebuck,* the plaintiff lawyer John McCann told me that the photos I shot of the burned two-year-old child played a significant part in reaching a three million dollar judgment in 1987 that set a precedent for raising gas hot-water heaters eighteen inches above the floor. There were many others for even larger awards, but this one was the most satisfying.

I have been able to have all these experiences because I am not a racist and I was taught to judge people by their character first and foremost, lessons I learned from my father and grandfather. I never forgot two things my grandfather taught me–one very early in life and the other a few weeks before his death. One day when I was about six years old he said, "Get one of those gravel shovels, get all those rocks out of that truck, and put them into these empty roofing-cement cans. I want the cans sixteen inches apart and not one rock on the floor." About an hour or two later, when he came back to check how I was doing, it was all finished. He measured the distances between the cans, took out a dollar, gave it to me, and said, "Now you know what a dollar is worth."

The second lesson occurred when I was nineteen. He told me to get a blank piece of paper and write my name on it. When I completed the assignment, he said, "That is the only thing you will ever own. I worked all my life to make it something you would be proud to bear." Many times since that day, knowing who I was, and who went before me living honorable lives, saved me. I do understand what Alex Haley intended when he wrote *Roots*.

The one thing that I hope is different about

this book from the many others that are mostly pictorials is that I am retracing my entire seventy years in the Crescent City and sharing with the reader not just the visual records of what I have seen but the stories behind both the events and the people in the pictures. The hundreds of thousands of photographs I have taken over the decades have survived hurricanes, at least three flooded houses, a few burglaries, and many years of eating Lenfant's one-dollar "Gravy Sammiches" so I could buy film. Some have damage, a name or two may be misspelled, but the essence of this work is a look inside the world of someone who has spent a lifetime enjoying, preserving, and hopefully improving the "City That Care Forgot."

So let us retrace my journey. If you are a local, I think you will say, "Oh yeah, I remember that," and if you are a visitor or transplant, you might say, "Wow! I did not know that." Therefore, prepare to stroll down memory lane, and take our New Orleans traditions into a world that will surely need our enthusiasm, determination, love of life, and unconquered optimism.

No one can get through life without the support of those who believe in what you are doing and sticking it out over a lifetime. With that in mind, special recognition goes to Kathleen Calhoun Nettleton and Nina Kooij of Pelican Publishing Company for publishing this book that has been in the making since 1976. In addition, I must thank my father, George W. Richardson, Jr., for introducing me to photography in my earliest years and my mother, Rita Thorning Richardson, for demonstrating by her life's work that healing the sick and helping those who are less fortunate is the way to live.

I offer special thanks to John Kemp, Jan Villarrubia, Ben Smith, Jeff Fields, Marc Zavadil, Dr. William Schmidt, David Erath, Yvette Warren, Gerard Steubben, Bobbe Haller, Chief Charles LaDell (NOPD), and Gilbert Luke for forty-one years of believing in this project. I also thank Gregg Stafford, Leroy Jones, Dr. Michael White, Nicolas Gillet, Carlos and Patrice Valladares, Charlie Miller, Jean and Genevieve Hurel, Dr. Ed Frieburg, Dr. Klaus Lumma, Margie Shorter, David Mancini, Jimmy Bayard, Hugo Kuijpers, Joan Casey, and especially Lillian Boutte for their support. Finally, I owe a great debt to the New Orleans-based Threadhead Cultural Foundation for its generous grant that provided me with the technology to restore and make decades-old photographs of New Orleans musicians available for this book. These historic images have been given new life, thanks to the foundation. It is impossible to recognize everyone who has played such a vital part in keeping this fire burning, but you all know who you are. *Blow down the sky!*

Threadhead Cultural Foundation

A Fire in My

Lens

Chapter 1

My Origins and History

Armand J. Richardson

Not many people can point to a photograph and say, "That's the first thing I can remember seeing." I could not have been more than two or three when my father held me up over that developing tray and in the yellow light I saw for the first time the magical appearance of an image on a piece of photographic paper. Even more fascinating, this was my namesake, Uncle "Sheik," who had died in 1941, four years before I was even born. I think that moment, when I saw that sudden appearance of someone I would only ever know through photographs, imprinted me with a lifelong interest that carries forward even to this day.
1422 Kentucky Street, 1940, by George W. Richardson, Jr.

Making Pictures

When someone asks me, "How long have you been doing this?" I usually show them this picture and say, "For as long as I can remember." Giving a child tools, a musical instrument, and access to books and then letting them discover the joy of creativity seems like the best investment a parent can make.
3607 Clermont Drive, 1949, by George W. Richardson, Jr.

Armand Joseph "Sheik" and George W. Richardson

Portrait of "Sheik" and "Ike" in front of the sheet-metal shop on Kentucky Street. Sheik was only nineteen when he died the next year of kidney failure at Hotel Dieu Hospital on Tulane Avenue. George would soon be on Guadalcanal in the first wave with the Seabees First Battalion in August of 1942. He had volunteered for submarines but was put into the construction battalion, where his master sheet-metal skills could be best utilized.
1422 Kentucky Street, 1940

Hotel Dieu Nurses and Charity Nuns Praying in Courtyard

On December 7, 1941, the Japanese attacked Pearl Harbor. When news of the attack reached New Orleans, the feeling of shock and horror was quickly replaced with determination and patriotism. In this photograph taken that afternoon, we see the nuns and nurses kneeling on the pavement praying.
Hotel Dieu Hospital courtyard, December 7, 1941, by George W Richardson, Jr.

"The Living Rosary," Hotel Dieu Student Nurses

Hotel Dieu Hospital was located on Tulane Avenue and had a nursing school just across the street. On special holidays, the entire student body and Sisters of Charity would create the "Living Rosary" in the courtyard of the hospital. This picture was taken from the roof of the front wing of the building.
Hotel Dieu Hospital, three blocks west of Charity Hospital on Tulane Avenue, 1941, by George W. Richardson, Jr.

Jackson Square Scene
Jackson Square facing the Cathedral, 1941, by George W. Richardson, Jr.

Armand J. Richardson

Portrait done by the *City Hall Talk Magazine* photographer Joe Davi, to be published along with the Dawn Russo photograph. This was the first working day after the Howard Johnson sniper incident that paralyzed the city for two days—my first experience with being shot at while taking photos. It was not the last.
City Hall terrace, January 1973, by Joe Davi

Dawn Russo

First published photograph, 1972. The occasion was the "Tribute to Degas" by the Harvey Hysell Dancers at Delgado Museum. It was a cold and rainy day and I merely went inside to get out of the freezing rain. Little did I suspect that as the door opened to that small auditorium, a whole new direction lay ahead for me.
Delgado Museum, City Park, 1972

"Fairview"

While visiting with playwright Jerry Steubben and painter Dawn Bailey, to show my dance prints to their houseguest, Rene DeMagny (a fantastic artist from Beauvais who had watched the Nazis march through Paris when he was nine). At this stage of using an SLR, I was very unsure about whether what I was doing was really good or not, so I was seeking evaluations from those whose talent I could easily see for myself. Self-proclaimed "artists" bore me to my limit and I still never use that word when referring to myself. While Rene was going through the seven prints I had, we heard a band approaching on Esplanade Avenue. I ran outside just in time to get two pictures before they were gone. I had no idea who they were or what I was doing with the settings on the manual camera, but I gave it two tries anyhow. How ironic that in this one shot, Tuba Fats, Branford Marsalis, Joe Torregano, Leroy Jones, Wynton Marsalis, and Gregg Stafford were all visible. Not a bad "first shot" considering who is in it! Another door opening.
Esplanade Avenue, 1971

"First Prize"

Figaro Professional Photo Contest, 1972, taken in front of Patti Latter's house on Napoleon Avenue. My experience with the Pershing Rifles and the USMC enabled me to previsualize this shot. A 1.5 second exposure that caught all the movements in one image was the key.

Three Gulls into the Sunset

While waiting for hours to get the shot of the single bird flying into the sun that I had previsualized, I suddenly noticed a single bird coming from the northeast that was going to pass right in front of the sun. At the same instant, two more appeared in the viewfinder from beneath the sun, one from the southeast, the other from the southwest. As all three were converging into the sun, I concentrated on the one coming from the northeast. I could see the image forming up as surely as if I was directing the birds into the sun. Just at the instant the gull from the right was about to cross in front of the sun, it raised its wings, and in that 1/2000th of a second, it rose above the sun. I was sure it was a miss because there was no "blackout" of the sun as the bird passed in front. A week later after the film came back from the lab, this image seemed to be flying off the screen. This was the first picture I ever sold. John Tocho, Sr., one of the top engineers in the department I was working in at J. Ray McDermott, told me that I was "wasting" my time at McDermott and "should pursue a career in photography." John was one of those who helped convince me that I should "go for it." He was a great friend and benefactor who often bought me lunch so I could use my money to buy film. I think in the theater world, they call people like that "angels."
West End by Fitzgerald's, 1973

With Herman Leonard at Satchmo Fest

One of the photographers I have always admired and wanted to emulate was Herman Leonard. He is, in my opinion, the greatest jazz photographer who ever lifted a camera. I had wanted to meet him ever since I first saw his pictures of Miles Davis and Ray Charles. One day while at Satchmo Fest, I noticed a small table in a hall with Herman Leonard's book on it. As I looked through it, someone approached me and said, "That's a nice camera you have there. Do you do this professionally?" I answered that I tried my best, but it was nothing compared to what I was looking at in this book. Little did I know I was talking to none other than the great one himself! We had a good laugh and he offered to go shooting with me whenever I was in town, and of course, I accepted. Weeks later, after I had gotten to know Herman pretty well, we were out shooting on Decatur Street and he introduced me to some of his New York friends by saying, "This is Sheik. He's a colleague of mine." *Wow!* He sure made my year with that one. The point is, it's not about being famous or rich. It's about doing something you love and making people happy with it. Herman said, "I was not that great. I just had access." We sadly lost Herman in 2010. He moved to L.A. not long after he lost thousands of negatives in the 2005 flood, and I never had a chance to see him again. As it turned out, he had lived just ten blocks from my house for over ten years, and I never knew it. He was truly a great man who had no egotism in him. He was a role model for any aspiring photographer.
U.S. Mint, Satchmo Fest, 2004, photograph with my camera by Benny Jones

Johnny Donnels

The "place to be" was at Johnny's apartment above his Starving Artists Gallery on St. Peter Street, just up the street from Jackson Square. An entire wall was covered with pictures of the famous, the going-to-be famous, and the "who cares about being famous?" Johnny was a really funny and kind man who shared his success in life with all those around him. His photographs were my first inspiration to try to make a go at doing something I never thought I would but wound up doing anyway. He shared information, beer, and humor with any and all, and some of the best times I ever had in the Quarter were out on Royal Street below his balcony. We lost Johnny in 2010 but his pictures remain forever. He was just one great talent and a hell of a nice guy. He was famous for being the "sketch artist" for the NOPD and was recognized nationally for his excellent drawings that often led to the arrest of a dangerous suspect.
Starving Artists Gallery, St. Peter Street, 1985

Oh, When Them Saints!

When I was a kid *everyone* played some kind of instrument. It could be those little plastic flutes in the first grade or that trumpet someone had handed down to you. When the Saints came to town in 1967, it was the Olympics and World Series all in one. It did not matter if we won or lost; we were in the big time! So every Sunday the gang would show up at the house. Most brought beer and potato chips, and we all settled in for an afternoon or night of pure bedlam. In this image taken by a "most likely" intoxicated reveler with my camera, we see Francis, a tuba player who had been with the Berlin and Chicago symphonies; me on trumpet; Craig Hopkins on clarinet (a master's in electrical engineering whose real passion was the saxophone); Derrick Thomas, formerly drum-section leader at St. Aug, on bass drum; Donald Thomas on "cowbell"; and Big Al, sometimes on trombone. Behind them, partially obscured, are Larry Filiberto (beer bottle) and Bobby Eichorn (sax). The whole neighborhood would come out and march around the block after a Saints win. If the Saints lost, all the beer cans would stay on the front lawn for another week of mourning. Oh, what fun!
6026 St. Anthony Avenue, 1990

On Location

For four glorious years, my crew shot all the houses for the "Latter and Blum Home Show" on WDSU-TV. As part of that, we shot really large properties for *Great Estates* magazine using a Linhof Master GTL 4x5, the premier view camera in the world, with the finest Schneider and Rodenstock lenses. I never told the management, but I would have done it for nothing! Dreams come true sometimes. We shot over four thousand houses, and I did all the interiors, so we had a ball. This shot was a huge property up around the Louisiana-Mississippi border that took days to do. Unfortunately we were so successful that the show was no longer needed and the onset of digital pictures made view cameras obsolete.
Northern St. Tammany Parish, for Great Estates magazine, *1993*

The Gentilly Brass Band, 2016

I always wanted to make up a band from Gentilly that would be really professional in appearance and sound. After many years of trying to find the right formula, I hit upon the idea of mixing full-time professionals with working people who liked to play but did not have time to dedicate to rehearsals. The result is what you see here. This picture was taken at a benefit for two NOPD officers who were paralyzed from the waist down when they were shot on duty. The Bucktown All-Stars horn section graciously joined in with our regulars and the result was astounding. Dr. John, Rockin' Dopsie, the Bucktown All-Stars, Marcia Ball, and Jimmy Anselmo all participated in that show.
CBD, 2016

Inspiration

I met Claire at the Maple Leaf. She was a student at LSU Medical School, studying to be an occupational therapist. She had glaucoma, so she knew she was going to be blind. I took her to the museum in City Park to see the Rembrandt self-portrait that was on display, and we went to Fontainebleau State Park afterwards. I asked her to do a photo that would capture what she saw that day and this is what we got. I never met up with her again after my first showing on September 5, 1975, which she came to and could still see her own photo up on the twenty-foot-wide screen. When cataracts made me legally blind in 2004, I thought about Claire and hoped that surgeons were able to help her too. Thanks to the Musicians' Clinic and the LSU doctors, my sight was restored in the summer of 2006. I can now see as well as I could when I was ten years old. I went through the entire Katrina disaster seeing seven of everything, in what looked like a Degas painting in real life. Claire's courage served me well during that time and still does today.
Fontainebleau State Park, 1975

"I am forever grateful for being christened by the sounds, smells, beats, sights, and words of New Orleans that fill my eternal soul."

—Yvette Autin Warren, New Orleans native, author, and chef

Chapter 2

Historic Scenes

Canal Street Ferry at Sunset

I rode the Third District and Canal Street ferries every day for the first nine years of my life. I was literally carried across by either relatives or Irish grandma Thorning (county Cork) until I could walk and later on cross by myself. I shoveled coal into the boilers, rode with the captain up in the pilothouse, steered the ferry, and stood on deck with everyone as we listened for the big bell that was our signal to find the distant landing in the dense fog. The smell of steam on the river is every bit as fragrant as Chanel Number 5. I knew almost everyone in Algiers who rode those ferries every day, and I still say that I lived in Algiers, the Ninth Ward, and Gentilly. I was in all three places every weekday.
Top of LP&L building, 1974

Holt Cemetery

Some mistakenly call this "Potter's Field," but it's not. Located right next to Delgado Community College on City Park Avenue, this is where uncounted thousands have been buried. Buddy Bolden is in there and many others. I sometimes walked through there at night to drop off film at Moldaners Camera Store, and often I heard what sounded like voices singing along with the wind in the trees. I would walk very fast when that happened.

Holt Cemetery, City Park Avenue

Blessing of the Fleet

Bucktown was this little fishing village when I was young. It was a big thrill to be told, "We're going to Bucktown," because it either meant a great restaurant or picking up fresh seafood for that night's feast. The building was destroyed by Katrina in 2005 and the fleet was decimated by dredging of the Seventeenth Street Canal after the hurricane. Today a small fleet hangs on, but Bucktown is not that little village anymore. The house was known as Bruning House and was never rebuilt.
Bucktown facing west from the Bucktown Bridge, July 4, 1976

The Green Streetcars

Another New Orleans icon is the fleet of green streetcars. Rumor has it they were painted green during World War II to camouflage them. At one time they were all over the city and you could go anywhere for seven cents with a free transfer. After Katrina, all the new red ones were flooded, so when service was first restored, green streetcars rolled up and down Canal Street again after a very long absence. Decades before, in one of the worst decisions ever made, many of the original green streetcars were broken up and replaced by gas-guzzling buses. New Orleanians protested but as usual, the outside "know-it-alls" in Washington and Detroit prevailed. It later cost hundreds of millions of dollars to replace the tracks on Canal Street. If it ain't broke, leave it alone!

St. Charles Avenue by Loyola University, 2017

"My parents still live in the family home on Canal Street where I grew up. Dr. Stanford Beatty, the first chiropractor in the city, lived next door to us. I remember him shaking his head that gloomy day in 1964 when buses started lumbering past. He said, 'They'll be sorry! Gasoline's going to be too expensive to run those big things. Electricity's a lot cheaper. They're going to put those streetcars back; you'll see.' When the buses started rumbling down Canal Street, we could feel the whole house shake. Soon the ceiling plaster in the front bedroom cracked and fell and pieces started falling off the columns on the front porch. That had never happened before. The house was built in 1908. NOPSI (the transit company back then) paid for those first repairs. Then started the downward spiral of Canal Street. On the last day the streetcars ran, about five of us (we were sophomores in high school) went down to the streetcar barn on Canal and presented our offering of $13.18. We wanted to buy a streetcar. The men were amused but said no. How about a streetcar seat? No. Instead, most of our streetcars were chopped in half, the interiors beaten into splinters. Others were given to museums."

—Jan Villarrubia, New Orleans native and playwright

Waiter, Cafe du Monde

Before segregation was finally ended, the only waiters at Cafe du Monde were white males. This shot captures one of the most famous of local traditions, the de rigueur white socks. A well-known photo of Satchmo shows him in his splendid tuxedo, with trumpet and handkerchief in hand and his white socks showing. It's as New Orleans as "where y'at!"
Cafe du Monde, 1976

Ninth Ward Revisited

I spent a great deal of time at my grandfather's house at 1420-22 Kentucky Street. The sheet-metal shop was located there from 1912 until 1968 when the business was closed. The building still stands today, a testament to "doing it right," as do the slate roofs in this picture. It was taken after "Big Jim" Garrison ran for judge, and his election poster dominates the scene. That small black "thing" on the corner is one of the original "bumpers" that would keep a wagon wheel from going into the ditch. What makes this photo special to me is that I helped put the slate roof on several of those houses when I was ten years old, and they are still there. That storm nail sure does work!
Mazant and Burgundy, circa 1975

"Among all the photographs on my walls, the one that folks usually stare at the longest is of this rundown, working-class neighborhood in mid-seventies Bywater. They seem transfixed, but they also seem to be wondering why anybody would bother to take this picture. Was it the curious iron bollard guarding the corner? Was it that this declining block of New Orleans houses was a metaphor for the city itself? Or could it be that the rest of the picture was just the perfect background for Jim Garrison's political poster? Garrison's formerly high-flying career was at this point also in rapid decline, as he had recently lost his 1973 election for a fourth term as district attorney."

—Jeff Fields, New Orleans native

Kolb's

This was the first and best German restaurant I ever went to in the U.S. Going there with the draftsmen and engineers from McDermott was a high point of almost every week! Sauerkraut was a standard item at our Irish-German house and still is. Unfortunately Kolb's closed and is no more. My favorite place now for this cuisine is in Eschweiler, Germany.
St. Charles Avenue, 100 block

Merry-Go-Round

The "Flying Horses" carousel in City Park was one of the rites of passage for all the kids in New Orleans (if you were white). When the park was finally opened up in the '60s, everyone could ride. But as the years went by, things that were always "free" suddenly had fences around them (Pontchartrain Beach, for example), and without money, one was locked out. The tradition of providing free museums, symphony concerts for schoolkids, open access to the parks and beaches slowly ended. It's one of the things that really should become a priority again.

Flying Horses, City Park, 1983

The Mighty Mississippi

This photo was taken from high above the Crescent City Connection, looking westward. The city is called the Crescent City because it was built within the curves of the Mississippi River. What is significant in this photo is that off to the left is the Gulf of Mexico. Coastal erosion has eaten up an area as large as Delaware in the past half-century. The loss of those wetlands and cypress swamps means the tidal surges that form in front of a hurricane now will hit the city much higher, since there is little to knock them down as they approach. That's why the levee at the Old Beach has been raised from three feet in 1963 to twenty feet today. My pilot for this photo was Ted Lococo, who was John Schwegmann's personal pilot at the time.

1,000 feet above the Crescent City Connection, 1995

Roman Candy Wagon

Every kid in New Orleans would listen for that bell . . . and when we heard it, we'd run outside with our nickels to get some of that "saltwater taffy." We had no idea what is was made of and never cared. We just knew it was and *still* is good.
St. Charles Avenue at Audubon Park entrance, 1986

Steamer President

Steve Burke says it best: "If you live in New Orleans and you don't play an instrument, you missed the boat." One of the best views of the city was from the decks of the *President*. Often the ship had bands playing downstairs on the first floor, while hundreds of passengers rode on all its decks. We could hear that steam whistle every night from as far away as Gentilly. Unfortunately, the *President* was moved to become a casino and nothing ever came to replace it. New Orleans misses that boat!
Steamer President *from Canal Street Ferry, 1980*

Rest-a-While

During the many "near misses" New Orleans experiences during hurricane season, Bucktown floods. The Rest-a-While had the good vision to place a nice sofa outside so the pirogue riders could pass by and stop for a well-earned rest. But it "ain't dere no more."
Bucktown, 1983

Preservation Hall

Ever since 1962, Preservation Hall has been the mecca for jazz fans from all over the world. All the greats have played there to packed audiences since day one. No air conditioning, a few benches, incandescent lighting, and no amplifiers all make it the most authentic jazz experience in New Orleans. And no, Louis Armstrong was not born there, no matter what those "tour guides" try to tell you.
Preservation Hall, the day Tuba Fats was buried, January 18, 2004

St. Joseph's Altar

One of the oldest traditions in the city is that of the St. Joseph's Altar. Italian families spend months preparing for them and anyone is welcome to come, visit the altar, put their prayer requests in the box, and of course share an authentic Italian feast. It's customary to leave an offering that will be donated to the poor box at the church. This one is presented yearly at the residence of Catherine Famiglio Tangius in Slidell. The family moved out of the city as so many have since Betsy, the May 8th flood, and Katrina flooded their houses. As the city has expanded, the traditions have as well.
Slidell, 2017

The Clock at Holmes

Ever since D. H. Holmes put up their clock on Canal Street, it's been a New Orleans tradition to tell someone, "Meet me under the clock at Holmes's." Even after Holmes closed, the custom remained. Holmes had a "no questions asked" returns policy, gift wrapping, and delivery right to your home. It was not uncommon for employees to work there for their entire careers. It was a great store with excellent merchandise. It puts the mall stores of today to shame.

D. H. Holmes, Canal Street, 1992

The Zephyr

This was a landmark for fifty years until some idiot from Florida came here and got a $27 million loan to "develop" the Pontchartrain Beach site into "condos." All he did was blow up the Beach with a few thousand dollars of dynamite, take the remaining millions, and declare bankruptcy. So the children of New Orleans lost their playland, and we lost the "rite of passage" of riding the Zephyr for the first time when we were tall enough to reach the line on the wall. The Zephyr was the only cypress rollercoaster in the U.S., and it is etched in every New Orleanian's memory who was "of age" before 1983. That parking lot is where a *lot* of us learned how to drive as well!
Pontchartrain Beach, Elysian Fields at the lake, 1980

Chalmette Battlefield

Everyone who visits New Orleans should add this to their list of things to do. In January of 1815, a battle occurred in which the invading English army ran into Andrew Jackson, Jean Lafitte, and a ragtag army of mostly volunteers who used their cannons to defeat the greatest army in the world at that time. Jean Lafitte is credited with directing the cannon fire that decimated the British. The Americans were greatly outnumbered, but by relying on a levee they had built to place their cannons on, they literally blew the English to pieces. According to official records, James, George, John, and William Richardson were among the defenders of the city, along with eight others who shared my last name.
Chalmette Battlefield facing Pakenham Oaks, 1994

Little Woods Camp

Today virtually all of the camps are gone, but back in the '40s through the '70s, all New Orleanians had to do was drive just past where the Lakefront Airport is today and they were in Little Woods. Betsy took a toll, and Katrina finished them off.
New Orleans East, 1977

Par 3 Number 3 City Park

Here is another example of "if it ain't broke, don't to fix it." There was a championship golf course featuring a 600-yard par 5 as number 4 in City Park, until someone decided it was better to have the New Orleans Open played outside of New Orleans. This course featured towering cypress trees and lots of water holes. Now, just like with the streetcars on Canal Street, millions have been spent to recreate what was already there in 1955. This photo was taken at sunrise on a freezing-cold morning just across the street from Shelter 6, which is now part of a dog park.
City Park, 1975

Zulu Social and Pleasure Club

The original location was across from City Hall on Perdido Street. The club moved to Broad Street long ago and the sign has been moved as well.
Loyola and Perdido vicinity, 1972

Hibernia Bank Building

In the '50s, we were always told that no building in New Orleans could ever be taller than the Hibernia, at twenty-eight stories. WDSU put its first antenna up there because it was the highest spot in town. In World War II, spotters were up there looking for Japanese planes after Pearl Harbor. The building still stands, and the tower is lit up for whatever holiday is current. Just a few blocks away, the fifty-one-story Shell Oil building stands today.
Hibernia Bank Building, 2003

French Market

Back in the '50s, you could get five huge watermelons for one dollar, and when you did and came home, the whole neighborhood got some. This is when the market was primarily a true farmer's market, long before the term "flea market" was used.
North Peters Street across from the Mint, 1976

Walk of the Oaks

Just to the right side of the museum in City Park as you faced the river, this was the view before Katrina flooded the entire park with salt water. The oaks were exceptionally beautiful, and when it was foggy and cold, it looked just like this.
City Park in front of the museum looking towards the river, 1976

Steamer Natchez

The last remaining steamboat on the Mississippi, the *Natchez* sails twice a day and is a great way to view the city and the river all the way to Chalmette Battlefield. In the summer, the sunset offers a great photo opportunity. The steam calliope can be heard all over the French Quarter about an hour before sailing.
Riverwalk, 2009

Morning Call Blues

This is one of the greatest ideas to hit New Orleans in many a year. Morning Call is open twenty-four hours a day and is the best late-night spot in the city I know of. Parking is plentiful and free, the beignets are excellent, and the park ambiance is unbeatable. Just across the street is the Sculpture Garden, which is both free and excellent.
City Park Casino, 2017

Pontchartrain Beach Bus Stop

Every New Orleanian sooner or later wound up here, waiting for the Elysian Fields bus. It was a great place to "pass some time" while waiting.
End of Elysian Fields, 1994

Russell Stover Candy Store

Those deep purple/magenta panels above the awning were like a beacon to every kid in New Orleans. We all knew what treats were just inside those doors!
Canal Street right across from the Maison Blanche Building, 1975

Mardi Gras Fountain

This is a great place to hang out at the Lakefront. You can walk the tour around the fountain, looking at the logos for every Carnival krewe that ever was. This is occasionally the site of the Mardi Gras Fountain Soap Suds Festival, put on by some enterprising high-school class.
Lakeshore Drive just past Canal Boulevard, if you turn right when you hit the Lakefront, 1973

Mid-City Rock n' Bowl

First opened in 1941, Mid-City Rock n' Bowl remains in business to this day. Since it was on the second floor of its original location on Carrollton at Tulane Avenue, it did not flood, but circumstances caused a move up the street near the College Inn. The original lanes are installed and so are the mechanical pin spotters, so it's a great trip back to the '50s for those who enjoy the ambiance of a past time.
Corner of Tulane and Carrollton, 2005

Pitt Show

Before TV came in, New Orleans had scores of movie shows that often featured live "talent nights," and you could see a double feature for as little as twenty-five cents. Kiddie matinees on a Saturday afternoon were the norm, as there were "serials" that were ongoing week after week. *Rocket Man* was my favorite! The Pitt was a modern and elegant theater that was one of the last to remain active. This photo was taken moments before the wrecking ball hit that west wall. The boom of the crane is just visible on the left.
Elysian Fields catty-corner from the Surf Lounge and Ferrara's Market, 1995

"Jingle Jangle Jingle"

Every child in New Orleans knew who Mr. Bingle was. We could watch him in the big window at Maison Blanche on Canal Street and every day on WDSU. Created by Emile Alline in 1948, and brought to life by Edwin "Oscar" Isentrout, Mr. Bingle instantly became a part of New Orleans Christmas tradition. Kids just loved the little guy with the ice-cream-cone hat and holly wings. Fortunately we can still get Mr. Bingle dolls today!
Canal Street, 1998

"Don't Fence Me In"

Popp's Fountain was always free and open to the public twenty-four hours a day. It was one of my favorite places to shoot portraits for years. Then one day, there was a fence around it, with a padlock. It was a very sad moment.

City Park by the pumping station on Marconi, 1995

Chapter 3

DANCE

Harvey Hysell's "Tribute to Degas"

This was the very first time I ever saw ballet and the first time I was trying to use my first SLR, a Pentax SP500 with a Kalimar zoom lens, Tri x at 1600, developed in Rodinal. After developing in hot water and stopping the film in icy tap water, I inspected the film and saw nothing on it. So I threw it on the floor and let the cats play with it for weeks. One night I threw one of those negatives into the enlarger, set the timer for .1 of a second, and got this perfect print.
Delgado Museum Auditorium, 1971

Lelia Haller with Watering Can

Lelia was the second American to become a principal dancer at the Paris Opera Ballet in 1926. In 1928 Ms. Haller returned to New Orleans to open her studio in the French Quarter. She taught classes in classical ballet until 1982 and established a degree program in dance at Loyola as well. Today there are two studios that both bear her name and continue the Haller tradition. It was her evaluation of my first dance photographs that convinced me to continue with that subject in 1973. I owe her an eternal thank-you for her confidence in me and giving me access to her classes as she instructed me on how to properly photograph ballet.
Harrison Avenue studio, 1973

Delta Festival Production of Sleeping Beauty

Bobby Couret was the sound man for the theater. He arranged for us to use the stage one night, so I took the 4x5 view camera and got this shot. Those velvet curtains and theater lighting were just perfect.
Theater for the Performing Arts, 1976

Bobbe Haller

Ms. Bobbe was Lelia's daughter. She followed literally in her mother's footsteps and became both an excellent dancer and teacher. Ms. Bobbe continued evaluating my photographs and helped me to improve over the forty-four years that I knew her. She touched and influenced thousands of lives with her lifetime dedication to the dance.
Uptown studio, 1975

Daniel Breaux and Claudia Dumestre Dancing at Satchmo Fest

This was always my favorite couple at any event where Gregg Stafford or Mike White were playing. I saw Daniel and Claudia at Economy Hall for the Michael White concert and spoke with him as he went second lining by in front of the stage. Little did I know that would be the last time I saw him smiling and enjoying life to the fullest. He was a true "good timer" and is sadly missed by all who knew him.
U.S. Mint, 2002

Tanya Henriques Kinnett

Tanya is a most remarkable dancer. She can do classical ballet and character with excellence, grace, and style. She puts in the endless hours of class, rehearsal, and teaching that it takes to be true to the Lelia Haller tradition. She does the sissonne with a precision and perfection that inspired me to call it the "Tanya." In this picture from the Ballet Louisiane production of *The Nutcracker*, she performs it with a radiant smile that can be seen from the very last rows. She and Dawn Russo have inspired me since that very first "Degas" photo in 1971.
Jesuit Auditorium, Saturday performance, 2015

Four Ballerinas

Lelia Haller studio, Canal Street, 2016

Ivy Fitzgerald

Ivy Fitzgerald performs the echappe in the Lelia Haller studio production of *Paquita*.
Tulane Dixon Hall, 2016

"Being part of the Lelia Haller Ballet tradition means so much more to me than the costumes or the curtain calls. It means that I am taking a path many before me have danced. It means I can always be inspired by the women who have been through the school before me. Today, when we dance, we aren't just dancing for ourselves but for everyone in the LH Ballet family. When I started ballet, I had no idea how much it would mean to me in the future—that I would make such great friends, be so inspired by everyone around me, and dance for something greater than myself."

—Ivy Kate, native New Orleanian and ballerina

Tribute to Degas

"Arabesque" by Virginia Quinlan, backstage before the performance.
Tulane Dixon Hall, 2016

Shannon Rodriguez

Wearing Ms. Bobbe Haller's original dress, Shannon performs the "Spanish" dance in *The Nutcracker* to perfection. Shannon was a student of Ms. Bobbe Haller and is skilled in ballet, tap, and jazz. She has danced in New York with Steps on Broadway, is an attorney, has five children, and teaches ballet and character dance at the Canal Street studio.
Jesuit Auditorium, 2012

The Flowers

Each year the Lelia Haller studio in Covington performs the "Waltz of the Flowers" in the Ballet Louisiane production of *The Nutcracker*. Each year one dancer is selected to be the "rose," and this particular year it was Alya McMillan.
Jesuit Auditorium, 2016

Eleanor and Ian

New Orleans natives Eleanor and Ian Carney perform a beautiful finale as the Sugar Plum Fairy and the Cavalier in the Ballet Louisiane production of *The Nutcracker*. Ian and Eleanor have created their own company, the Lightwire Theater, which has performed all over the world.
Jesuit Auditorium, 2012

"Jump for Joy"

The Mari Meade Dance Collective in New York has roots in New Orleans and particularly with the Lelia Haller studios. Mari was a student of Ms. Bobbe Haller before moving to New York and establishing her own very successful and innovative company. Featured in this photo are Allison Beler from Metairie (in yellow) and Rachel Rizzuto from Chalmette.
Brooklyn Arts Exchange, 2012

Chapter 4

GRAND MARSHALS

Booker T. Glass with Shannon Powell

The first jazz concert I ever photographed using a Leica SL2 was the first Jazz Roots Concert at the Rivergate. I was wandering around the French Quarter when I saw a parade headed down Canal Street towards the river. When I saw Fats Houston riding in a mule-drawn carriage I decided to tag along and have been doing it ever since. I did not know Shannon yet but soon would! Shannon is one of the all-time great drummers and I am delighted to have seen his career bloom and continue on. His red beans and rice are legendary! In this picture of Shannon with Booker T. Glass, I see both the majesty of the Grand Marshal and the passing on of our traditions to the next generation. All over the world, the New Orleans Grand Marshal symbolizes the Crescent City and preserves the dignity and character of New Orleans.
Rivergate, circa 1973

Fats Houston, First Jazz Roots Concert

When we got to the Rivergate I realized that Fats was unable to second line because he had crutches and needed assistance to get up on the stage. Since I had been watching him all my life, it was a very sad moment for me. However, once that magical music started playing, Fats was *up* and leading the audience from the stage on his crutches. It was a great moment, when the nobility and spirit of New Orleans were manifested in the determination and power that Fats had. The Grand Marshal is indeed the perfect representation of what New Orleans is and we are fortunate to have had so many greats in the past who carried this tradition forward.
Rivergate, circa 1973

Fats Houston, Louis Cottrell Funeral

Having seen Fats unable to walk at the first Jazz Roots Concert, I thought that my chance to get a suitable photograph to preserve his vibrancy and charisma was never going to happen. When Louis Cottrell died in 1978, I went to the funeral, since I had gotten to know him when I was "brought in" by Gregg Stafford, Danny Barker, and Herman Sherman. The Onward Brass Band was one of the very finest and Mr. Cottrell was a pied piper with his sweet clarinet sound. To my astonishment, as I navigated through the huge crowd in front of the church after the service inside, a miraculous vision stood before me. It was Fats and he was leading the funeral procession without a cane! Visitors have to realize that a jazz funeral *is* a *funeral* and not just a party. Fats' mere presence often would convey that to locals and visitors alike.
Gentilly, 1978

"Smiley" at the Louis Armstrong Birthday Party

I never knew him by any name other than "Smiley." He was a fixture at every festival, concert, and second line as well as on Bourbon Street, dancing in the street with the tap dancers. Smiley had a trick where he would take out his false teeth and use them as part of his routine. This photo was taken on Satchmo's declared birthday of July 4, and whether that's historically correct or not, if "Satch" said it, it's good enough for me!
Jackson Square, 1976

"Pork Chop"

"Pork Chop" (Oliver Anderson) was another of those longtime fixtures in the French Quarter, with his lively outfits and superb tap-dancing style. Half of the vaudeville act of "Pork Chop and Kidney Stew," he was a friend of my father's, so I got to know him when I was very young. When Henry Dudley died, Pork Chop got to live out one of his lifelong wishes, to be a Grand Marshal in a jazz funeral. The tuxedo he's wearing was Henry's, as were the sash and top hat. The smile tells it all. Not long after we had another sad day, when Pork Chop died as well.
Henry Dudley Funeral, Rampart Street, 1985

King Richard Matthews

For most New Orleanians, Richard became the icon who represented the city once Fats was no longer able to Grand Marshal. I got to know him over a thirty-five-year period and he was always the perfect gentleman and professional. Few realize what it takes to be a real Grand Marshal. The creation and maintenance of the umbrellas, suits, and sashes are never-completed works of art. Grand Marshals are in front of the band for a reason. They clear the crowd and look out for potholes in the street that the musicians might trip on. Without the Grand Marshals, I don't think the spectacle of the second line would be nearly as interesting.
Tuba Fats' wedding in Armstrong Park, circa 1994

Ellyna Tatum

Ellyna was a nurse at Charity Hospital who often would work on her days off to help patients who needed her care. She was a lovely person whom I got to know even before I worked with her son "Duffy" at Model Cities in the late '60s. She was a great singer; her rendition of "Closer Walk" would bring even the most unruly crowd in Jackson Square to respectful silence. Ellyna was also a pioneer in being one of the first women to be a Grand Marshal.
Basin next to the auditorium, 1985

Gabby's First Appearance

As sometimes happens at the Jazz Fest Economy Hall Tent, a new talent just emerges from the audience to steal the show. So it was with Gabby when she picked up an umbrella and was so good that the band called her up on stage to electrify the audience. She's all grown up now and still leading second lines and singing.
Economy Hall, circa 2002

Oswald Jones and Trixie Minx

The Grand Marshals of New Orleans now have a growing tradition of female members, Trixie being one of them. Both Oswald and Trixie are always immaculately costumed and give great performances. In New Orleans you can pretty much "be what ya wanna be" and find a place to do that. When Nico Gillet first conceived the idea of having Trixie join Oswald in leading the Treme Band in Ascona, it proved to be a brilliant innovation that has caught on over there and here as well.
Ascona Jazz Festival, 2016

"Doc Mancini"

"The Doc that Rocks" is Grand Marshal for the Down Undahs, the Renew Brass Band from Eschweiler, Germany, and the Gentilly Brass Band. Doc can carry it off in "tie and tails" or in shorts and T-shirts. He's truly one of New Orleans' greatest "Yats" and the most devout Saints fan imaginable. Having been a vice president of an "old line" bank, he got excellent experience in "taking care of the money" and still does! An East Jefferson "Warrior," he got a lot of "Yat" experience in high school.
"Down Undah Field" by the Superdome, 2015

"Kitty Kat"

Kristina Steinke has been a professional dancer, costume maker, and artist all of her life. She's equally talented at all of these, so it was natural that New Orleans became her "second home" after she lived and performed here for years starting in 1971. I first met her at Tucks 1996, where she was dressed in her "Kitty Kat" persona, and eventually we wound up with the marching club in Tucks year after year. You can see her every Mardi Gras Saturday leading the band in front of the marching club and stopping constantly to have her picture taken with the legions of children who flock to her naturally. She made this costume and it's a *big* hit on Mardi Gras Day as well.
Tucks parade, Napoleon Avenue, 2008

Wesley Jammin' in Red

The unproclaimed "King of Gentilly" is none other than Wesley Schmidt. He's one of those responsible for the Pair-O-Dice Tumblers, Kosmic Debris, Easter Oyster Hunts, and MOMS. He also has led the Storyville Stompers since their creation in the early '80s. He is a master costume maker, photographer, and mixologist and was doorman at all the first MOMS balls, when anyone could get in no matter how sparse their costuming was. A smudge of face paint was usually enough to get you in! Wesley can sometimes be found at Snug Harbor, where he manages one of the best music venues on Frenchmen Street. His favorite song has to be "It Ain't My Fault."
Economy Hall, Jazz Fest, 2014

Henry Dudley

The first time Gregg Stafford told me to "go talk to that guy over there" was at the Louis Armstrong birthday party in 1976. I went up to him and told him what Gregg had said, and he replied, "Have you ever seen a hearse followed by an armored car?" Being somewhat under the influence of certain celebratory substances such as a Hurricane or two, I went back to Gregg and told him what Henry had said. Gregg then said, "Go back over there and see what else he has to say." So I did, and Henry said, "If you can't beat them, outlive them." We both roared with laughter and thus began a friendship that lasted until Henry's death in 1985. Inside that top hat he wore were signatures of people such as Muhammad Ali, Queen Elizabeth, Dwight Eisenhower, Louis Armstrong, and many more. Henry had polio when he was young and walked with a limp. When he had to find a way to make a living that would not require two healthy legs, he wisely picked up an umbrella and never looked back. In becoming a Grand Marshal, Henry succeeded beyond anyone's expectations. He and Fats Houston became the symbols of New Orleans and left us a legacy that will remain forever.
Slidell, 1982

Grand Marshal in Black

The tradition of the jazz funeral exists because of the reverence and true emotions that are the foundation of the jazz funeral. This image of Norman Dixon from the very first jazz funeral I photographed captures that perfectly. Norman is credited with saving the second-line tradition in the '70s.
Oak Street, 1975

YMO Grand Marshal

The Young Men Olympian are one of the oldest of the marching clubs that parade year round in the "City That Care Forgot." These social clubs exist so that when a death occurs, a proper funeral can be held for the deceased. They are in every part of the city.
Jackson Avenue, 2004

Chapter 5

Mardi Gras and the Eternal Party

It's Carnival Time!

New Orleanians are already in Mardi Gras mode on January 6, when the first Carnival club has its ball. The Twelfth Night Revelers have kicked off Mardi Gras season since 1870. For me the real start of Carnival is when the "Mardi Gras trees" bloom. Their actual name is Japanese magnolias but we know them by both names.

Popp's Fountain, City Park, 1994

The Butcher Cut Him Down

Shrove Tuesday is the day before Ash Wednesday. The Rex parade always has the Boeuf float at the number four position. The song "Didn't He Ramble" is tied to this tradition and is played at jazz funerals immediately after the interment of the deceased. The excesses of Mardi Gras are followed by the abstinence of Lent.
St. Charles Avenue, 1983

Mardi Gras Tree

All over town, trees, fences, front doors, cars, and businesses display purple, green, and gold—the official colors of Mardi Gras. Sometimes it's taken to extremes!
Marigny, 2014

All Hail Dreux

Capt. David Labayan leads the assembled marchers in the annual cheer before the Krewe of Dreux takes to the streets of Gentilly. Mardi Gras takes many forms and is held all over the city. In Gentilly, the Krewe of Dreux parades from the Peoples Avenue Canal up Dreux Street, to St. Roch, to Prentiss Avenue. Usually several hours of serious beer drinking are followed by a timbales-led procession to the Bacchus Lounge. Often the queen's reviewing stand is a Dempsey dumpster, and on at least one occasion she fell into it. This is a truly local krewe that has not changed over the years.
Peoples and Dreux, 1979

Zulu

Each year Zulu precedes Rex down St. Charles on its way to the Zulu headquarters on Broad Street. In times past, Zulu had no set route, and to find it was a lot like "chasing Indians or Bone Men." Today the hugely popular Zulu parade follows a set route but has been known to be a little tardy in starting.
St. Charles Avenue, WDSU stands, circa 2001

Smile

A heavily disguised former queen of Tucks stands on Mardi Gras Day with the Mad Hatter and the Mouse from *Alice in Wonderland*. Chaos reigns supreme, and anyone can be whatever they choose to be for one day!
St. Charles Avenue, one block from Jackson Avenue, circa 2010

Little Mardi Gras Clown

Fat Tuesday is always for the children first and foremost. This little clown was at Patty Latter's house that morning and was the picture-perfect child.
Napoleon Avenue, 1972

The Corner Club

Every year since 1918, the Corner Club has marched down St. Charles Avenue on Shrove Tuesday. Brilliant satin costumes, beads for the crowds, and a good time for all.
St. Charles Avenue at First, 1998

The Marching 100

Anytime the St. Augustine Band appears in a parade, the crowds explode with excitement. In 1968, the St. Aug Marching 100 broke the color barrier by marching in the Bacchus parade. It was a great moment in New Orleans history and I was lucky enough to have seen them on St. Peter Street behind the cathedral. A breakdown stopped the parade for eighteen minutes, and the band played "Bourbon Street Parade" for the entire time. I knew I was a witness to history at that moment when the crowd erupted in cheers and there was dancing in the streets. I understood then that a new day had come to New Orleans.
Morpheus parade, 2016

St. Augustine Marching 100 Alumni

In 2017, Rex did a magnificent thing by having a contingent of the 1968 Marching 100 ride on one of its floats. In a time of constructive change in our city, this went a long way towards mending fences and recognized that St. Augustine High School has given so much to America as well as to New Orleans. Words cannot express the joy of seeing my old friend Dwight Richards riding in the Rex parade with brother Purple Knights. Bravo, Rex; Bravo, St. Augustine!
Canal Street, 2017

MAKE BBQ NOT WAR

This refers to one of our great trumpet players and entertainers, Kermit Ruffins. It would not be a bad idea to elect Kermit to office. No one would be hungry for very long! New Orleanians have a great sense of humor, and Kermit does his part to keep the blues away.
Marigny, Mardi Gras Day, 2004

Trojan Orpheus

Orpheus is one of the best night parades, with lots of flambeaux, fiber-optics, throws, and celebrities riding in the parade. They travel the traditional Uptown route, and Harry Connick, Jr., gave a gift to the city by cofounding this krewe.
Tchoupitoulas Street, 2016

Have Camera, Will Hunt

David Erath stands at the corner of Royal and Frenchmen, headed out with his trusty camera to seek Mardi Gras treasures. A Gentilly boy made good, he owns and operates the Christmas shop on Decatur when he's not out searching for prizewinning photos.
Frenchmen Street, 2007

Tucks Royal Court

Known for its irreverence and satire, Tucks has grown from a few college students getting kicked out of Friar Tuck's Bar for lighting flambeau napkins and marching around inside the bar to a full-fledged krewe with over 1,700 members and some of the largest floats of any day parade. The highlight of the Coronation Ball is the introduction of the maids, which in itself is reason enough to attend.
Marriott Hotel, 2015

The Dukes of Mardi Gras

Dukes and captains usually ride on horseback in their parades. Their identities are often kept secret, as part of the mystique of Mardi Gras. There is a law requiring that float riders wear masks as well. One never knows who is behind that mask. It could be your lawyer, your hardware-store clerk, a surgeon, or a bartender. So when one waves, wave back!
Proteus, 2016

Happy Birthday to Me!

This lucky masker has a million people all celebrating her birthday. That's not a bad way to get lots of throws and maybe a few Zulu coconuts too.
Canal Street, 2014

Kosmic Debris

This is the most appropriately named krewe in all of Mardi Gras. No membership, no dues, no rules . . . just show up, bring an instrument (even if you can't play one), and join with the Tumblers. You can then roam the French Quarter playing such "traditional" tunes as "Sex, Drugs and Rock and Roll Is What I Want to Do." This group is led by Alan Langhoff, who usually orchestrates the Debris and Tumblers into total chaos on Mardi Gras Day. In 1979, with the police on strike and the mayor telling everyone to "stay in their homes," the most "logical" thing for Kosmic Debris to do was march from the Dream Palace at noon into the Quarter. March with them for a while and you will know how they got the name!
Iberville Street, 2016

Tucks Marching Club

Liz, Tommy, Marcelle, and Roy warm up before the big walk down St. Charles. I omit their last names to protect the guilty. One of the most popular parts of the Tucks parade each year as they meander through the crowds is handing out favors and throws to a very appreciative audience. Each year their trademarks of an outlandish theme and spectacular costumes get more extravagant. The Riverside Ramblers always are great too.
Napoleon Avenue, 2017

NOFD on Parade

Without our firemen and police, there could not be a Mardi Gras. It takes a very special person to run into a burning house, and these guys don't hesitate to do it. Hats off to them all.
St. Charles Avenue, 2015

Capt. Robert Reichert

Bobby was the instigator of the infamous "flambeau incident" at Friar Tuck's that led to the mega-organization that Tucks is today. In this shot from 2014, Bobby is being symbolically arrested for violating the city ordinance for littering the streets with tons of tissue that winds up in all the oak trees on Napoleon and St. Charles. He managed to talk his way out of the arrest and promptly led his merry band of Tuckians to do their papering job. While Bobby won't be leading the parade anymore, he surely will be remembered whenever anyone sees St. Charles blanketed with tissue. He was famous for his special "salute" that was freely given as a sign of friendship.
Napoleon Avenue, 2014

Biodegradable

A motion was put forward to the City Council to outlaw the throwing of "tissue" by "certain" Carnival krewes. Apparently not everyone appreciated the Krewe of Tucks' sincere efforts to "beautify the Avenue." Once it was determined that Tucks was being environmentally conscious and using biodegradable paper that would disappear the moment it was rained upon . . . the issue evaporated like bourbon or champagne at a Tucks ball.
Napoleon at St. Stephen's Church, 2017

Zulu Big Shot

Every Carnival organization has captains, dukes, a king, and queen . . . but Zulu alone has the "Big Shot," who is the power behind the thrones. Splendidly attired and riding high above the crowds, he presides over the distribution of the world-famous Zulu coconuts and throws.
Zulu parade, St. Charles at Poydras, 2001

Oh How He Rambles!

Drake Morvant leads the Riverside Ramblers as only he can. Often accompanied by "Kitty Kat" or his "lieutenants," Drake lights up the spectators with moves that the Rockettes could not try. He is a previous king of Tucks and one of the highlights of each year's parade.
Gallier Hall, 2010

Flambeaux Proteus

This "old-line" organization formed in 1882 and still uses the original float chassis. Unlike the "super krewes" that use huge floats, Proteus has remained traditional and has original flambeau torches in the parade. For its 100th anniversary, a mule-drawn float led the parade exactly as one had in its first year. One of my favorite parades, it's always colorful and features great bands. I used to walk in it with Terry Mars, who was the parade organizer.
Napoleon Avenue, 2014

Queen of Morning Call

Brooks Zitzman, queen of Tucks in 2015, displays her fantastic "Queen of Hearts" gown at the Morning Call in City Park. Brooks is a graduate of the Tulane School of Social Work and daughter of a former king of Tucks, Tommy Zitzman. Brooks was a magnificent queen who brought smiles to all who saw her that day. She currently lives in the Washington, D.C. area but participates by video phone call and shares champagne with her fellow office workers and the marching club on the Napoleon Avenue neutral ground just before the parade starts.
City Park, 2015

MOMS

MOMS was created by a group of Gentilly Yats as an antidote to the "uppity" and exclusive old-line organizations. The first two balls were held at the Franklin Avenue Legion Hall, with holes in the floor and a cross-section of New Orleanians. There were no dues, membership rules, or committees; it was just something to do rather than go to Bacchus. To get in, all you had to do was have some kind of costume, which could be as simple as a little face paint or a mask picked up at Schwegmann's, Goodwill, or Farrell's Drug Store on Clematis. As the party grew it moved to Tipitina's, and then to the hall down in St. Bernard. Even then there were no tickets or memberships. Earl King played the first ball, and later on the Radiators became the regular band. The big moment of the ball was when the Tumblers took over at "half-time" and a raucous second line went on until everyone was totally "blown out." Jazz legends such as Leroy Jones, Gregg Stafford, and Larry Talerico participated in the early years. Some years the Krewe of Dreux parade was held that afternoon and everyone piled into cars and headed straight to the MOMS ball immediately afterwards for what would be a full day and night of celebrating.
VFW Hall, St. Bernard, 1983

9th Ward Marching Band

Until Hap Glaudi made the Ninth Ward famous, it was an almost invisible part of New Orleans. Okeanos started their parade at Poland and St. Claude, but beyond that the only landmarks were the Florida and Desire housing developments. My aunt Kate lived in the Florida projects, so I got to spend some time there. My grandfather lived on Kentucky Street and operated the sheet metal and roofing business there from 1912 until 1967. So you can imagine how great it was to see the 9th Ward Marching Band coming down the street well over 100 strong.
Napoleon Avenue, 2013

The Queen

The Krewe of the Queen started in 1974 when Coleen Salley gathered a group of her friends and decorated a shopping cart as their only float. The group carried on that tradition until Coleen's untimely death, but her son David continues the house party that the members still flock to on Mardi Gras Day. Coleen is remembered as an educator, storyteller, and author of children's books. She is dearly loved and missed by all who knew her, as her heart was as big as the French Quarter she loved.
St. Peter Street, 2014

Strike Up the Band

The "Roots of Music" band was started by Derrick Tabb, snare drummer for the Rebirth Brass Band, after Katrina. The band succeeded in getting instruments and uniforms for young musicians who wanted to play after the storm. They gained national attention for the excellent work they have done in bringing music to the lives of New Orleans' children.
Napoleon Avenue, 2008

Down by the Riverside

Steve Burke, the closest thing to Sam Butera playing today, jams with Dr. Ed Frieburg on Mardi Gras in 2006. It was probably one of the most important second lines in New Orleans history, as it sent a message to the world that "we're still here and we ain't goin' nowhere." Two people were instrumental in bringing the city back who sought or took no credit for doing so. Ed, as head of the Tulane Pediatric ICU, was the only staff physician there 24/7 for several months after the hurricane. Steve brought back his extra-special talent and gave meaning to so many who needed that in the "dark days."
Post-Katrina Mardi Gras, Decatur Street, 2006

St. Charles Avenue Strut

Every year Carnival krewes parade down St. Charles on their way to a ball that always follows. Capt. Lloyd Frischhertz and twice-queen Marcell Frischhertz prepare here to join the Tucks Marching Club for the annual trek to their Extravaganza. Unlike the riders on the floats, marchers mingle with the crowds and hand their beads directly to the recipients. This is especially popular with the children along the route, since they don't have to compete with the older and taller parade goers. Lloyd and Bobby Reichert started the krewe in 1969 and the krewe has paraded every year since.
St. Charles Avenue, 1994

Katrina Be Gone

Leroy Jones sends a message to the entire world: "We're *back* and we are going to *stay*." John Boutte can hardly believe his ears and that note is still echoing around the French Quarter. It's impossible to adequately relate how important it was for us to be out there on Mardi Gras in 2006. It would be many years before anything resembling "normal" would return, and we all had devastating damage to our homes and possessions. Without the music I don't think we could have made it. Can you imagine it was *six* weeks before I heard James Andrews playing on Decatur Street in the French Quarter? I think the flood made us realize that what we have can't be copied, can't be impersonated, and can't be stolen. We have something in us that goes back hundreds of years, and it sure came out that day in the deserted streets of the French Quarter.
Decatur Street, 2006

"Mardi Gras 2006 was by far the most memorable Carnival Day ever for me and how much more special being surrounded by friends, revelers of the Krewe of St. Anne, and faithful New Orleanians committed to returning to the city they love, despite the disaster the majority of us experienced when our levee system failed in the wake of Hurricane Katrina practically six months before this annual celebration. It was so good for my spirit to see John, Ray, Sheik, all my colleagues with the Storyville Stompers Brass Band, and all the folks who decided not to give up on our beloved Crescent City. Mardi Gras 2006 was an exhibition of strength, perseverance, resilience, love, faith, and hope. The band played on."

—Leroy Jones, New Orleans native and professional trumpet virtuoso

Who Dat?

As long as I have been alive, this phrase was used in all kinds of situations. In this case it's "what dat?" because the costumes defy labeling. If you want to enjoy Mardi Gras to the maximum, buy, or better yet *make,* a costume and hit the streets. Be what or whom you ever wanted to be and get out there. I have no idea who or what these two are depicting, but they surely had a great time that day. John Kennedy walked the streets of New Orleans one Mardi Gras Day in the '40s. I wonder how many people knew who he was? That's the fun—you never know who you will see or share a drink with on Fat Tuesday!
Royal and Canal, 2017

Dreux Baby Doll

Local WWOZ radio personality and queen of Dreux in 1978, Sally Young rides in the New Orleans Baby Doll Ladies parade on Mardi Gras Day. Sally's radio show features only traditional New Orleans jazz, which makes her one of the key persons keeping that tradition alive. When she's not being a "Baby Doll," she's helping the music community by working on benefits and traveling to the Ascona Jazz Festival in Switzerland to send back reports from there.
Bourbon Street, 2017

Dancin' in the Streets

Mardi Gras Day is so special! Here we see the queen of Sheba dancing with Sir Frederick Astaire Bojangles XIV, the dancing doorman at the Monteleone Hotel front entrance. It's the "Greatest Free Show on Earth," we used to say in the golden age of the '50s and early '60s. Back then the oil companies were really surging forward and we had great public schools, parks, streets, transportation, and NORD to keep the kids out of trouble. I always tell people, if they take away segregation then New Orleans in the '50s was the "Greatest Place on Earth to Live." Thankfully, segregation is a thing of the past and we're making giant strides to build an equal and fair society on the local level. We're in hard times now—Katrina surely did not help—but with the spirit this city has, I do believe "We Shall Overcome."
Royal Street, 2017

The King of Carnival

I have a dream that one day Rex and Zulu will ride together and make up the greatest Mardi Gras parade ever seen. We've made giant strides since the Second World War ended and have a long way to go . . . but when I saw that special float with the St. Augustine alumni band members riding in Rex, it was a moment I won't ever forget. My family has been in this town since at least the early 1800s. Some of my ancestors were at the Battle of New Orleans. All of my uncles were in the military and a few saw the flag raised on Iwo Jima. We've survived war, depressions, floods, fires, and epidemics. There's only one reason that they came and stayed, and that was the lifestyle and cultural traditions. I am reminded of Sam Cooke's "A Change Is Gonna Come" and surely it will. Bravo, Rex! Bravo, Zulu! Bravo, St. Augustine Class of '68! Y'all done good!
Canal Street, 2017

The King's Jesters

The Krewe of Rex started as a satirical jab at the visit to New Orleans by the Grand Duke Alexis Romanoff in 1872. Rex has maintained the highest level of artistic design and execution ever since.
Canal Street, 2017

The Russians Did It

We all just *knew it,* didn't we? They built those substandard levees, bribed Mayor Nagin, designed the "Carrollton Mistake," and planned the World's Fair. I'm glad they finally "fessed up" to it all.
Royal Street, 2017

I Need a Band

It's the Sunday night before Mardi Gras—the busiest, most insane weekend of the year in New Orleans—and the phone rings at ten o'clock. "I need a band," the all-too-familiar voice of Lloyd Frischhertz said. "*I need a band!*" "Lloyd! It's Mardi Gras Sunday. Everyone's already booked. I can't think of anyone who could do it." "Well, just see what you can do. I need a band on the title float tomorrow afternoon for Tucks." So I picked up the phone and started dialing. Much to my amazement, every person I called said, "Sure! For Tucks? Sure!" So we showed up on Monday at Napoleon and Magazine and started climbing up on the first float in the parade after the queen's float. We had a hard time because we had to climb over bags of throws to get up on the top deck. Lloyd came by and asked, "Y'all need anything?" We said, "What do we do with all this stuff?" "Just get rid of it!" he replied. So off we went: our bass drummer, Stephen Guerdon "Banjoboye" Smith, with a broken wrist, Dr. Ed Frieburg on sax, and everyone else either hung over or already blown out from the parties on Saturday and the nonstop parades on Sunday. And so it went . . . we threw, we played, we drank a little, we threw some more, and we played. It was a parade to remember! *Lundi Gras, 2014*

Flambeaux

All Along the Riverfront

The original flambeaux were made in 1872 by James Richardson to light up the night parades for Comus. There were at one time as many as 700 of them but over the years the number of the original "torches" has dwindled to less than 50. Kerosene is used with a gravity-fed system, so the torches are very reliable and safe when maintained correctly. The reflectors were stainless steel and gave off a very bright light. The sticks were originally mahogany. When the torches were lit up at Magazine and Napoleon, or Magazine and Jackson for some parades, we could see the glow in the sky from as far away as St. Andrew Street, where our family used to meet.

Napoleon Avenue, in front of St. Stephen's Church, 2015

You Lit Up My Life

The original torches were all four burners. As time took its toll on the originals, a two burner was created with the same basic design. They are lighter and therefore made it easier for "carriers" to make the route. The modern versions are very well designed and built with the same or better safety features as the originals.
Proteus, Napoleon Avenue, 2016

Sashaying Down the Avenue

The Krewe of Orpheus has regularly increased the number of flambeau carriers and given them a bright red tunic to perfectly complement the orange fire glow of the torches.
Napoleon at Tchoupitoulas, 2015

"My brother, Mike, and I begged long and hard, well, as long and hard as an eight and seven-year-old can, and my mother finally agreed to take the two of us to a night parade. Mardi Gras in New Orleans during the late 1940s, when mules still pulled the floats and the flambeaux lit up the night sky. I don't remember what the weather was like or how long it took the Canal streetcar to get from Mid-City to downtown, but I can remember the excitement and the anticipation of our first night parade. I remember a lot of walking but it was fun walking, watching, and listening. The streetcar let everyone out around Claiborne Avenue and our little legs carried us past the movie houses, the department stores, and the streets of the Quarter on one side of Canal and the streets of the Business District on the other, different street names on either side of the street. We found a spot in the middle where the streetcars usually ran and listened for the drums that would announce the start of the parade. We never let up on our mother with questions: when would the parade start? how long do we have to wait? Everyone was bigger than us and we wanted to see. Jumping up and down didn't help but it was fun and added to the excitement. At some point I was aware of my mother talking to someone. It was her cousin Will and a friend of his. We learned later that Will and his friend, Billy, attended Tulane and played football. But that didn't really matter. What mattered was that they were big and could see and that was important. We wouldn't have ignored my mother's cousin and his friend so we probably asked them the same questions that we had been asking my mother. There were sirens blowing and thousands of people talking and laughing and then the sound of the bass drum off in the distance. I knew what that meant and the excitement grew. "It's coming, Mike; it's coming. The parade is coming!" The bass drum got louder, then the snare drums and the brass started to play. The next thing I knew I was on Will's shoulders and Mike was on Billy's and we could see. It was like we were giants and this was all happening for us. We could see the fire from the flambeaux from blocks away and anticipation grew. From there it all blurs together: the floats, the bands, the mules, the flambeaux, the smells, the sounds, hollering what kids, big and little, have yelled forever, "Throw me something, mister!" A seventy-five-year-old man remembers all that because the sights and sounds and smells still provoke that excitement, that feeling in the pit of the stomach, and the uncontrollable urge to jump for a pair of beads."

—Gerard Steubben, playwright and drug counselor

Proteus

Some of the Carnival krewes keep membership a closely guarded secret. All krewes are required to mask while on a float. Here a member of Proteus is directing the lighting of the torches and controlling the valves to ensure they are set properly. Usually someone dressed in this manner is a duke or captain of the krewe. There is a feature to this photo that one should look for. I won't reveal it since it's a "photo secret" that I am not allowed to tell.
Napoleon Avenue, 2014

Swearing Them In

In the "old days," the flambeau carriers were a lot less professional and the police would "swear them in" before giving them the torches. The bearers were lined up against the fence on the side of St. Stephen's Church and the dogs would sniff for drugs and impress upon all concerned that nothing "out of line" was going to be tolerated.
St. Stephen's Church, 1975

Strike a Box

When the torches are lit, there is a short time when the kerosene has to be regulated to achieve proper combustion. The burner acts as a "glow plug," so it has to reach operating temperature to ignite the fuel. The fire department is always present and ready to act instantly should anything even start to get out of control. I have never seen a torch blow up or burn uncontrollably in over sixty years of watching. Here we see the "drippings" being extinguished instantly.
Napoleon Avenue at Magazine, 2017

Good to Go

To a "first-time observer," it may seem as though this torch is completely out of control, but actually it's a freshly lit torch that has almost reached operating temperature. In a matter of seconds, it will be operating perfectly and adding magic to the night parade.
Napoleon Avenue, 2012

New Orleans Cyclotron

One of the most amazing aspects of the flambeaux are the dancing and spinning of the torches in time with the music of the marching bands. It's as much a skill as the arabesque turn in ballet and not for the timid! It's never a good idea to throw money into the street for the carriers. The proper thing to do is hand them dollar bills or even larger if you can spare it.
St. Charles Avenue near Gallier Hall, 2013

Like My Father Before Me

This is one of the professional carriers who has been doing this since he was in high school. Carriers take great pride in what they do, and it's not a "walk in the park" by any means when that can on top of the "stick" is full of kerosene. So please treat these culture bearers with the respect they deserve for making our night parades unlike any others in the world. They can use a water bottle too.
St. Charles Avenue in front of House of Bultman, 2012

Candygurl

This is the first woman that I ever saw carry a torch. It was Candy's first Mardi Gras; she saw an advertisement for flambeau carriers and decided to give it a try. The experienced carriers welcomed her and gave her all the information she would need to be successful. She finished the parade and came back to do more.
Proteus, Napoleon Avenue, 2017

Vulcan's Messenger

Traditionally, carriers would wear a white smock with a hood on it to act as a protector should fire drip down. The handkerchief is more to filter out the smoke than hide identities and does not indicate any kind of criminality. The police carefully check out all the carriers to make sure they are not intoxicated or criminals. After all, each torch has a gallon of fuel and weighs enough to do real damage if dropped or thrown. Usually all of the carriers are known to the police from previous years and there is a camaraderie between them.
Canal Street, Bacchus parade, 2008

Cha-Ching!

Many modern carriers develop their own persona that plays to the crowd and gets extra tips. Some go to great lengths to create their unique signature look. This is the "bling king" of flambeau carriers.
Proteus, 2017

Mysterious Masker with Torch

Many of the carriers create their own identity in order to gain more tips from the parade goers. If you go out to shoot these torches, be *very* careful not to back into one. They are not intrinsically dangerous but the fires are hot.
Napoleon Avenue, 2016

"Ghost of those who continue to traverse lands to which we bind our souls; therein lies the tie that binds us all to the infinite heritage of those we leave behind and those with whom we continue our journey."
—Robert Kauhane Lua'I, native Hawaiian

Tear Down Your Wall

How ironic that the place where slaves were forced to hold their celebrations (Congo Square) is often locked on Mardi Gras morning, thus preventing the Bone Men from continuing their tradition of both remembering and honoring those who lived their lives deprived of the rights that we all take for granted today. I think this is one of the greatest contributions the Bone Men make to New Orleans tradition, as the years pass and the number of those who lived in segregation dwindles. "Do not enter" had a particularly powerful and ironic meaning for Zohar Isreal that morning. The front gate to Armstrong Park was locked to those who came in peace to remember the souls who labored and lived during that terrible time.
Main entrance, North Rampart Street, Armstrong Park, 2015

You Next

Just imagine being awakened on Mardi Gras morning by this "terrifying" creature! It's all done in great good humor and residents in many parts of the city await the Bone Men's arrival with great anticipation. There is no set route and no timetable . . . to see them is either a great stroke of luck or taking the time to get out there early and hope they come. Here, Big Chief Albert Morris is about to wake up the neighborhood!
Treme near the Backstreet Museum, 2013

Passin' It On

One of the most important things about New Orleans tradition and culture is passing them on to the next generations. Without that, the music, the food, the flambeaux, the streetcars, the joy, and the fun that make the Crescent City perhaps the most unique city in the world do not exist. Camarre and Dee are already part of a tradition going back to 1819 and will be carrying it forward for generations yet to come. If you come here to visit, take the time to find out from the locals, who are "always willing to share" what those traditions are, and respect them so we can keep our city as creative and fascinating as it has always been.

Marais and St. Bernard Avenue, Mardi Gras Day, 2013

Tomb of the Unknown Slave

In 1992, lay rector Bill Savoy suggested to Pastor Jerome LeDoux that a shrine or garden plot commemorate the suffering and atrocities committed upon Africans brought to the United States in chains. With the cooperation of many volunteers, the design was created and the monument built. It was dedicated on October 30, 2004, and blessed by Archbishop Alfred Hughes. Dr. Frank Minyard played "Just a Closer Walk" and a large crowd attended the dedication. Each year the Bone Men return to the shrine, as they also do to a spot in Congo Square where slaves were auctioned. Any visit to New Orleans should include a stop at the "Tomb of the Unknown Slave" to pause and contemplate the evil of slavery and why we must eliminate all forms of racism and discrimination from our world. Here Royce Osborn, leader of the Congo Square Bone Gang, pauses on Mardi Gras Day to pay respects to all those who lived under that terrible curse of slavery. As with the jazz funerals, it's important that the significance of this ritual done by the Bone Men each year be understood and respected. A large plaque is on the church wall adjacent to the shrine and deserves a full reading. Ironically, the street facing the shrine is named after a Confederate brigadier general who became governor (1888-92) after the Civil War. He refused to intervene in 1891 when a mob gathered at the Parish Prison in New Orleans and thirteen Italians were lynched.
Governor Nicholls Street, one block from North Rampart, 2015

The Black Indians

Guardian of the Flame

My grandfather lived in the Ninth Ward on Kentucky Street, and we would drive down to visit him on Mardi Gras morning almost at sunrise. I recall riding over the overpass by the train yard and seeing a lone Indian walking towards Canal Street. I was ecstatic having seen a *real* Indian for the first time in my then very young life. My father patiently explained that this was a very special kind of Indian, a Black Indian. Apparently he knew the Big Chief. Many years later, I was walking down Broad Street on what may have been a very early Super Sunday and all the Indians were coming by in small groups or even just by themselves. Far off in the distance I saw a bright orange figure approaching and I loaded a fresh roll of film into the Leica. When the Indian got close, he stopped and looked right at me, and I am pretty sure that was the same Indian Chief I had seen so long ago. I found out later his name was Donald Harrison, Sr., and he was masking for the first time as a Guardian of the Flame after years of inactivity. I don't think I can ever make another photograph of a Black Indian Chief as powerful as this one. A copy hangs in his wife's house in the Ninth Ward, just a few blocks from where my grandparents lived, and where I saw that "Blue Indian" in the early '50s.
Broad Street by the pumping station, 1989

Big Chief Tootie Montana

I met Tootie at the jazz funeral for Earl King in front of Gallier Hall. Tootie noticed I was wearing a band hat and carrying a trumpet and a camera. We started talking and he told me, "If you want to know anything about masking or the Black Indian tradition, I am your guy." That was absolutely the truth. Anyone I talked to told me that Tootie was the spokesperson for the Indian tribes and had been instrumental in putting to rest the violent side of the tradition from the past. Instead he inspired the "who is the most beautiful" symbolic "battle" that probably saved the Black Indian tribe tradition from self-destruction. Tootie masked for over fifty years and died giving a passionate speech in a raucous City Council meeting where the Black Indian tradition was facing a possible end. Tootie taught me the differences between an "Uptown Indian" and a "Downtown Indian." One was three-dimensional, the other used stones and feathers as their style.
Gallier Hall, 2003

Pink Indian Behind Krauss

My first experience photographing Black Indians was on St. Joseph's Day in 1973. I was on the way to an assignment at the Royal Sonesta when I saw the long line of brilliantly costumed Indians approaching. This first experience has led to a lifelong fascination and interest in preserving the tradition by documenting a part of New Orleans culture that tourists seldom see.
Basin Street, 1973

Black Indian on Jackson Avenue

This was my first venture into Indian Country, in 1973. I wish I knew the tribe or name, but things were happening fast and there was no time to ask questions!
Jackson Avenue, circa 1973

Big Chief on Jackson Avenue

After hearing that the place to find the Indians was on Jackson Avenue, I headed down there around 9:00 A.M. on Mardi Gras Day. The advice was good and I ran into a lot of different tribes and had quite a day chasing after them all afternoon.
Jackson Avenue, 1974

Indians on Mardi Gras Day

That first time in the Jackson Avenue area, I had no idea what the details were about the structure of the tribes or the connection to Native Americans going back to the times of slavery. I worked with Leon Anderson at City Hall in the Model Cities Program. Leon had been a Mardi Gras Indian and he was the first one to explain to me what was really behind the tradition. I never knew the names of any of the Indians or anyone else in that part of town, but that did not stop me from going out there and finding out that I was more than welcome. No surprise there!
Jackson Avenue, 1973

Jazz Fest Indian

Now that the Jazz Fest has several stages where Black Indians perform, it's becoming a lot easier to find them. The Congo Square Stage is a good place to start.
Jazz Fest, 2013

Yellow Indian on Loyola Avenue

This is another glorious example of craftsmanship and style. One has to move fast when photographing Black Indians, because those suits are *heavy,* and once they start running, it's hard for them to stop. Getting run over by one of these guys is just like having the entire LSU line mow you over on the sideline at Tiger Stadium. Been there, done that too!
Loyola Avenue, circa 2004

Big Chief Donald Harrison, Jr.

Who can ever forget that first Mardi Gras after Katrina? Those of us who could be down in Treme that morning in front of the Backstreet Museum kept waiting and waiting for Bone Men or Indians to appear. After a very long and apprehensive wait, a single Bone Man appeared. More hours passed and finally the Bone Gang came around the corner sometime around 11:00 A.M. or noon. Chief Donald Harrison, Jr., came down the street. He was the *only* Indian I saw that entire day. I think we all knew that we had to do whatever we could to keep the city alive in what was a very dark time.
St. Claude Avenue, 2006

"I moved to New Orleans in 2003, lured by the promise of the 'Big Easy.' My visits there each year had enough rich memories to help sustain me through another year of the mundane in your average American city.

But living there was more challenging once you got below the surface. Grittier, not so Easy.

Yet the memories there will always be the zenith of my life. They are everywhere for the taking—if you immerse yourself. The wealth of layer upon layer of cultures, of centuries. A depth of experience that, each time it enters you, encompasses your entire being. And always the music. Music everywhere. The finest music heard anywhere I have been on this earth.

A defining moment. After Katrina. An empty city had their first Super Sunday. Mardi Gras Indians scattered far from home. Their feather and bead suppliers flooded. Trying to gather remnants from strange sources to make a 'pretty' costume. Desolate streets devoid of color that were once their homes. Nothing at first. And then they came one by one—maybe a dozen, maybe twenty. Not more. The colors reverberating against the emptiness as they danced. The air silent from the missing music and the absent crowds. Yet we witnesses saw they had made their stand. They and this great city could not be defeated."

—Debra Perlan, Colorado native, art and furniture sales representative

Flag Boy

Each tribe has its own organization. There is some variance but generally every tribe has a Flag Boy who goes out ahead of the Chief and shows the colors of the tribe. There are others like the Wild Man and the Spy Boy that also have specific functions to perform.
Broad Street at the Pumping Station, 1995

Big Chief Gerald

Everyone knows Gerald French as the son of George French and the grandson of Papa French, but few know him as "Big Chief." The Black Indian tradition has already been international since the Meters joined forces with George and Amos Landry in 1975. George and Amos were members of the Black Indian tribe the Wild Tchoupitoulas, and that combination took Europe by storm. Big Chief Gerald French is not just one of the best drummers in the world but he's equally comfortable in his "suit" on the "bricks" in Ascona.
Ascona, 2008

Chapter 6

MUSICIANS

The Magician

"Uncle" Lionel Batiste was and remains one of the all-time greatest bass-drum players in New Orleans history. Uncle could do more with a bass drum than any two others combined. His movements were so fast that getting a shot like this could take hundreds of tries. Uncle was really Benny Jones' uncle. And from that, Lionel adopted the whole world as his own. When Nico Gillet asked me to be Lionel's "bodyguard" in Ascona, Switzerland, I spent ten days witnessing the "greatest show on earth" as he worked his magic both on stage and in person with everyone he met. He was always impeccably dressed and courteous and had a humor that was so dry it often went by many. I sure do miss Uncle, and the six or seven jazz funerals he got attests to his enormous worldwide popularity.
Jazz Fest, 2006

Young Tuxedo Brass Band

Ever since my father used to take me to see the jazz funerals at Claiborne and Esplanade, I always wanted to be in one of those brass bands. Back then, such a thing was unheard of because of something called "Jim Crow." Around 1973, I ran into a remarkable trumpet player named Gregg Stafford, and he started inviting me to come with him to funerals and gigs. Through Gregg I met just about everyone in the jazz world and eventually lived out my dream of playing with the Tuxedo Band. Not only that, I got to run the streets with all the living legends and never looked back.
Fair Grounds, 1979

Southern

This is the "Bayou Bowl," with Grambling and Southern. Since my mother was in charge of all the Red Cross aid stations in Tulane Stadium, I worked on the mini ambulances that would go up into the stands on the back ramps and pick up patients. For the Soul Bowl, I was put on "break" so I could go watch the bands. To my surprise, the police opened the gate onto the field and suddenly I was out there listening to what sounded like the biggest pipe organ in the world. The Southern Jaguar Band was featuring the Platters, so they laid their instruments on the ground and put on white gloves, and the entire band and stadium sang, "Smoke Gets in Your Eyes." Doug Williams threw what must have been a seventy-yard pass for a touchdown to top it all off! Since that day I have been a Grambling and Southern fan.
Tulane Stadium, '70s

Amanda Happening!

Everett Link, the legendary bass man who started out with Ronnie Kole, comes running. "You've *got* to come *now!* It's *happening!*" "But Everett, I am over here in the Economy Hall shooting the Jazz Hounds and I just can't leave!" The next thing I know, Everett is dragging me to the Kids Tent just a few hundred feet away. As we near the tent, I hear this crowd going crazy and a red-hot Cajun band stirring up the pot. When we get inside, we see this very young and very small bundle of dynamite burning up her fiddle and singing up a storm. It really was a happening: Amanda Shaw in her very first Jazz Fest appearance!
Kids Tent, 1999

Charlie Miller, Blowing Down the Sky!

Charlie is one of the all-time greatest New Orleans trumpet players to ever pick up a horn. He has an amazing style and perfection of tone and technique that put him in the same class as Al Hirt and Louis Armstrong. Charlie is a graduate of Manhattan School of Music, served four years in the navy, played at Carnegie Hall when it meant something, and played in Broadway shows and with Dr. John's original band. Though he is largely unknown outside of the music world, say his name and people in the know start smiling.
Ascona, Switzerland, 2008

"Year: 1945. Tiny, fragile, three-room shotgun house, family of five, in the woods of Metairie (rabbits and snakes galore). I started playing music on my mother's old-time washing-machine hose. One day I didn't put the hose back on in time, and she found out when she emptied the machine (rancid water everywhere). Soon a man gave me a beat-up trumpet that his son used playing cavalry. Learning songs from the radio, two years later at age fourteen I joined a band doing gigs in Louisiana Cajun towns. I was the only one under fifty in the band. When R&B was born, I got involved in this new fiery rhythm in New Orleans. Then four years of navy and some savings there, and it's on to a world-leading music conservatory in New York City, Manhattan School of Music.

After the first year at Manhattan, I was broke, so the school gave me a full scholarship for the rest of the time. It was heaven being in the school orchestra, surrounded by the rich sounds of strings and French horns in such masterworks. My trumpet lessons were at the Juilliard School. My instructor, William Vacchiano, a world-leading trumpet teacher, had been the major instructor at Juilliard for many decades."

—Charlie Miller

Dr. Ellis Marsalis, Jr.

A living legend, Mr. Marsalis has been playing piano ever since high school when he switched from saxophone to piano. Patriarch of one of the great jazz families of New Orleans, he has been a huge influence in the jazz world. Unrecognized for far too long because he did not specialize in either traditional jazz or R&B, he came into prominence playing with Cannonball Adderley, Nat Adderley, and Al Hirt and has always been a highly respected piano player. Devoting much of his life to being an educator at the New Orleans Center for Creative Arts, UNO, and Xavier, he was awarded an honorary PhD by Tulane University in 2007.
Covington High School, 2014

Irma!

Ever since she was nineteen, with her first record in 1959, Irma Thomas has been the "Soul Queen of New Orleans." A string of local and national hits have illuminated a lifetime career of bringing it all home to the city. With style and grace, Irma has been a New Orleans favorite for decades.
Tipitina's, 2014

Big Noise in Economy Hall

Dickie Taylor and Everett Link perform one of the most challenging feats on drums and bass. Everett fingers the strings and Dickie taps them with his sticks playing "Big Noise from Winnetka." Everett is a Fortier High School alumnus who was an intrinsic part of the Ronnie Kole Trio along with Dickie.
Jazz Fest, 2003

Patrice Fisher

A classical harpist with degrees from UNO and Tulane, Patrice ventured into the world of jazz in the 1980s and has developed a style that is totally unique. She spends a great deal of her time doing benefits to bring harp music to students in both New Orleans and Guatemala. Her Latin jazz group Arpa is a regular at local festivals such as Jazz Fest and French Quarter Fest. She has toured in Germany and Central and South America. On this particular day, Chiko and Rogerio from Aracaju, Brazil, were the featured guests.
Jazz Fest, 2007

"New Orleans is one of the few places on the planet where it is possible to survive as a Latin jazz harpist with original music. There are so many cultures here that exist side by side and complement each other. I try to reflect this multiculturalism in my music. Since most of the land area in our city has been reclaimed from the swamp, it is precious. We build our houses close together and we get to know our neighbors. This closeness makes for an interesting gumbo of influences. Sheik Richardson has spent fifty years capturing many of the cultural images that are uniquely New Orleans. Natives can recognize our beloved traditions in Sheik's work, and the rest of the world can marvel at our quirkiness."

—Patrice Fisher

Slide, Frog, Slide

Waldren Frog Joseph was one of the greatest trombone players ever to come out of New Orleans. I knew "Frog" when I was very young since he knew my father way back there in the '40s. Frog played with Big Joe Turner, Earl King, Smiley Lewis, Louis Cottrell, Paul Barbarin, and just about all the great jazz men from New Orleans. He was another of our patriarchs, with three sons who are all jazz musicians, Kirk, Gerald, and Charles.
Jackson Square, 1975

Kirk Joseph

Son of the great "Frog" Joseph, Kirk has created a tuba style all his own. Kirk plays with a power and style that are both funk and traditional and can fill up a street or auditorium with sound without any amplification. He is an all-around professional and a great friend.
Tipitina's, 2006

Just a Moment

Roland LeBlanc started out very young playing guitar with Mac Rebennack in 1959 and singing such hits as "Junko Partner," "Just a Moment," and "I Was a Fool." Roland was a down-to-earth guy who would play with garage bands to help them learn how to play "New Orleans," as we call it. Charlie Miller said that "Roland had the best voice I had ever heard" and Aaron Neville is quoted as saying, "He was the singingest white dude I ever heard." I concur with both those comments. Roland was immensely talented and had no ego. He was a Gentilly guy if ever there was one.
Musicians' Alumni Association, 1995

"Roland 'Stone' LeBlanc—my friend, the singer, musician, entertainer. He captivated audiences with talent and personality that filled the room. When I worked with Roland, on or off stage, or developed arrangements in my converted studio/garage, his musical excellence radiated. He was always nervous before going on stage, but you'd never know it after three notes. Musicians lucky enough to know him personally usually agree that you never caught him making a mistake while performing. He was a master of covering mistakes. He once told me, 'Son, when you play a C chord [on piano], it doesn't matter if you use your fingers or your elbow, as long as it's a C. The audience doesn't know, and it just gets jazzy. They think you're bluesing it up.' He was right!"

—Jimmy Bayard, New Orleans native, drummer, vocalist, and writer

Sidney Schaff

I met Sidney in 1976 when Willie Gunther and I were working as "undercover" cops at UNO. That in itself should get a lot of laughs from the Luigi's crowd. Sid was lost one day and I answered a call and wound up driving him home in the police car instead of arresting him. I became friends with Sid and ended up buying a house in the 6000 block of St. Anthony Avenue, where he had lived. He was a painter and sculptor and did a "one-man show" at Luigi's that featured a "Karen Ann Quinlan" sculpture. Sid played with the Tumblers and always had a good time. I think playing the horn was the one thing he really liked to do the most.
MOMS Ball, 1982

Buddy Bolden's Blues

Here Dr. Michael White plays on the steps of Buddy Bolden's residence on First Street near South Liberty Street. Buddy was the earliest jazz musician and bandleader in New Orleans. He was a sensation in the late 1890s and early 1900s, when he began improvising popular and dance music using the black hymn and blues singing styles on his cornet. Dr. White got his PhD from Tulane University, has a tenured chair at Xavier University, and is the leading jazz historian in the world today. His renditions of "Burgundy Street Blues" and "High Society" are classics.
2307 First Street, 2008

Blue Lu and Danny Barker

I met Danny via Gregg Stafford and he in turn introduced me to Leroy Jones. I spent many an afternoon sitting in Danny's living room listening to stories and talking about his work bringing traditional jazz to the young people. Danny was with Satchmo when he went to Chicago and New York and told many stories about what had to be the experience of a lifetime. The red beans and rice at the house were extraordinary too! There was a gold record on the wall of their house, given by Maria Muldaur, with the title, "Don't You Feel My Leg." They were wonderful people all the way. So much of the jazz music of the '60s until the '90s was directly due to his work with the Fairview Baptist Church brass band.
Jackson Square, 1993

Onward

Back before Katrina, there were many "old line" brass bands, each with a very distinctive sound. They had regular members, wore traditional uniforms, and were always spotlessly clean and neat. They showed up on time, played with perfection and spirit, and were never "under the influence." In this photo, the great Louis Cottrell is pictured with Teddy Riley and Chester Jones on bass drum. Chester's son Benny leads the Treme Brass Band and is now also playing bass drum at this point in his career. Louis's tone was just beautiful and Teddy would lay in what I would call "Chicago progressive" riffs. This was one of my all-time favorite bands.
Jackson Square, 1975

Kid Treme

It's not often that someone from Ascona, Switzerland, becomes a certified "Yat." Nicolas Gillet is one such person. As artistic director of the Ascona Jazz Festival, he has been a frequent visitor to New Orleans and brought our best jazzmen to his festival. An accomplished drummer in his own right, he's played and marched with Treme and many others, including Bone Tone in the Tucks parade. Nico has always done a lot for New Orleans, but after Katrina and the manmade flood, he did exponentially more. Ask anyone on the traditional jazz scene and they will tell you what an incredible thing he has done in helping to keep the music alive. It was Nico who first invited me to Ascona to give a forensic presentation about the flood and who brought me to the hospital when I was having the first of two "widow maker" coronaries. He is a great friend of New Orleans and anyone he knows. Bravo, Nico!
Tucks parade, 2010

"In 1989, I went to New Orleans for the first time in my life. Thanks to Lillian Boutté, I was introduced to the real values and tastes of New Orleans: the family (a big one!) getting together in the kitchen after a working day, talking, making jokes, and waiting for Gloria's gumbo. The best! What a joy! And then go off and listen to some good music.

During one stay, thanks to her connections and her love, I got to participate and play at Erving Charles, Jr.'s funeral (R.I.P.). A sad occasion that changed my life. At the time, I didn't know this great bass player. Now, I will always be grateful for what I learned that day. Bob French brought a snare drum and sticks for me to play and I started parading with some of the greatest musicians in town: Herlin Riley, Dr. Michael White, Tuba Fats, Lucien Barbarin, and many others. It was a huge and very respectful parade. It seemed to me that the entire city was there; everybody loved and appreciated Erving.

In that moment I realized how deep the culture in New Orleans is, the meaning of a parade, and, in a larger sense, the meaning of music. That's when I understood that the primary function of jazz is found in the culture of brass bands.

Thank you, New Orleans, and thank you, Lillian, for letting me be part of it. As a tourist or as a music lover, for a funeral or for Mardi Gras, it doesn't matter. I found a richness and a mix of sensations, between sadness and joy, that my friend Sheik helped me to keep alive and grow over the years.

One year after Katrina, when the real values of things and music were at risk of a substantial change, Sheik took me by the hand and told me: 'After all the hard times we have to go through, we still want to dance, get together, and feel the power of our music. Come and celebrate with us.' So there I was for Mardi Gras 2007!"

—Nicolas Gillet

Emanuel Sayles

To many people, New Orleans is known as a trumpet mecca, and surely we have many great players both present and past. What many do not know is that the presence of great trumpet players creates the need for great "sidemen" who often are virtuosos in their own right. Emanuel Sayles was initially a viola and violin player, but he taught himself to play guitar and banjo. His strumming looked as fast as a hummingbird's wings and he became known as "the cat who could play anything." His favorite TV show was *Lawrence Welk*, but when it came to jazz, no one was better.
Jackson Square, 1977

It's a Hurricane

At the French Quarter Festival in 1999, I read the program and saw "Hurricane Brass Band" listed for the stage way back by the aquarium. So I ran from the Mint all the way to where the Canal Street Ferry Landing is to see Leroy Jones' Hurricane Brass Band. When I got there, there were these white guys with band hats that said *Hurricane*, but that was definitely *not* Leroy! So I stayed, shot a few pictures, and headed back to the Mint. Little did I know then that when Katrina came, it was the "Hurricanes from Netherlands" who were the first to offer assistance and they continued to do so for years to come. Before they were called the "Hurricanes," they were called "King Zulu's Brass Band." I had a chance to go play with them at the "Bubble" in Maastricht and it was quite the riot!
French Quarter, 2007

Gregg Stafford

There are not enough words to describe the "hound dog running" we have done since I somehow met Gregg in 1973. We were both just starting out, he in music and me with the cameras. Let's just say that we've had some fun. We would run around with Herman Sherman, Fats Houston, Henry Dudley, Kid Sheik Colar, and just about everyone who was into the music scene in the '70s until today. Through Gregg, I met just about everyone I know today and even had some chances to play with him and the Tuxedo Band on occasion. We're still going strong, though I have slowed down a few notches. As leader of the Young Tuxedo Brass Band, he's doing a great job of preserving the traditions exactly the way Herman Sherman and all the previous leaders of the band would have wanted. Ask him about the "Blue Runner" and get ready to laugh!
Tulane Student Union, 1978

A Night to Remember

It was the day that Armstrong Park had been dedicated, and that night the "World's Greatest All-Star Jazz Band" was going to play on the *President* along with Lionel Hampton. I had to save up for two weeks to get the tickets but when the time came, we were on the boat sitting way in the back behind a column where we could not see the stage. I remember that Herman, Teddy Riley, Charles "Blue Runner" Barbarin, James Tocho, Sr., Henry Dudley, and Placide Adams were all at this one table. Chris Clifton came over and he was fuming! "They don't even have a place for Lucille to sit." I was in an especially generous mood, so I said, *"No problem!* We'll make some room where y'all can sit." So Chris came over with these two well-dressed ladies with silk scarfs and warm friendly eyes and we all resumed our hydrating with Schlitz and Miller. I wound up sitting next to this one lady who was very friendly and asking all about where I came from and what I thought about the ceremonies that day. I told her I could not see much since I was way back in the crowd but I did not care since I was only there to honor Louis Armstrong, whom I had seen as King Zulu and heard when he played at Loyola in the '60s. I went on and on about how important he was to New Orleans and how much everyone loved him. She asked me if I really meant all those nice things I said about Louis and I said, "Of course, he is an inspiration to every kid in New Orleans who wants to be just like him." She paused and said, "I am really glad you said all those things about Louis. I am Lucille Armstrong; that's my husband. Louie would have liked you." After I picked myself up off the floor, she asked, "Would you be so kind as to show me around the French Quarter after the concert so I can revisit the places Louis took me?" Of course, I did, and the letter she sent me afterwards appears here. Who could ever forget such a night?

The President, *1980*

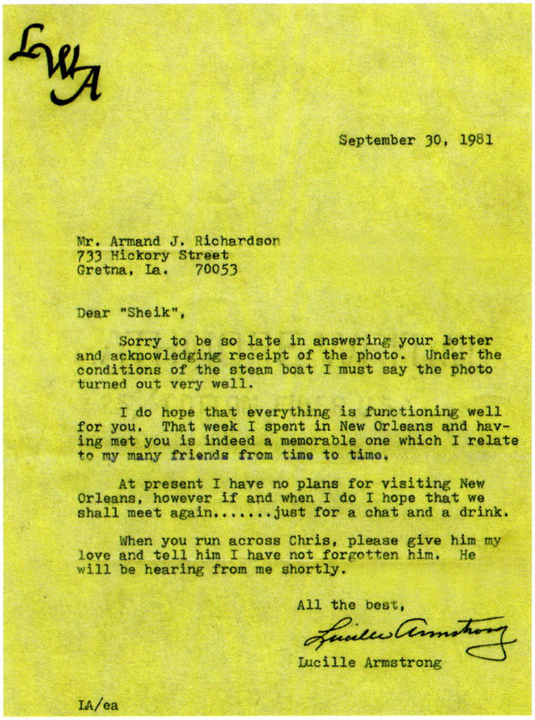

LWA

September 30, 1981

Mr. Armand J. Richardson
733 Hickory Street
Gretna, La. 70053

Dear "Sheik",

Sorry to be so late in answering your letter and acknowledging receipt of the photo. Under the conditions of the steam boat I must say the photo turned out very well.

I do hope that everything is functioning well for you. That week I spent in New Orleans and having met you is indeed a memorable one which I relate to my many friends from time to time.

At present I have no plans for visiting New Orleans, however if and when I do I hope that we shall meet again.......just for a chat and a drink.

When you run across Chris, please give him my love and tell him I have not forgotten him. He will be hearing from me shortly.

All the best,

Lucille Armstrong

Lucille Armstrong

LA/ea

Chris Clifton

Chris was from Detroit but wound up traveling with Louis for seven years on the road. Charles Barbarin used to say, "When I hear Chris playing, I close my eyes and I hear Louis Armstrong." It's true, Chris can emulate that sound and style to a *T*. When I did some shows on WWOZ when it first opened, Chris did a ninety-minute interview/show with me. I still see him and always listen for those incredible slurs he can do.
French Quarter Fest, Bourbon Street, circa 2002

Sure Would Like to Meet Charlie Miller

It's not often when a photo matches perfectly a high point in one's life. Dr. John (Mac Rebennack) had played the Cor Jesu 1963 prom at the Hilton Inn on Vets. Roland LeBlanc was in that band also. Ever since that night I had always wanted to meet Charlie Miller. I had seen him from a block away at Jazz Fest blowing down the sky at a Dr. John show but just never managed to run into him in person. So there I was with Leroy Jones doing the usual rounds at French Quarter Festival on Bourbon Street. I was telling Leroy how I wanted to meet Charlie Miller and Leroy (who had moved around behind me in the crowd) says, "You want to meet Charlie Miller? OK. Turn around." At that moment of turning, I clicked the shutter and there it is: two of the greatest trumpet players in the world, right there on Bourbon Street having a few beers. This is one of my all-time favorite photos of two of my all-time favorite people.
Bourbon Street, 2005

"Talk about trumpet legends of New Orleans, and I'm not tooting my own horn here. What an honor to have a Kodak moment with trumpeter/musician Charlie Miller. He just happened to be among the audience checking me out with my band at French Quarter Festival. Charlie has performed with the who's who in the music industry, yet maintains a humble spirit. I appreciate the compliments he gave me and the band that day."

—Leroy Jones, New Orleans native and trumpet virtuoso

Ninth Ward Jump

This is Easter Sunday in the Ninth Ward, just a few blocks from Kentucky Street where I spent one-third of my younger life. Herman Sherman, leader of the Young Tuxedo Brass Band, had invited me to come along for the parade they were playing. Within sight of the two-story house I had "helped" build at 1422 Kentucky Street, Sherman told me to start playing. The first song I ever did with them was "Over in the Glory Land," which was normally the first song they played while going to "pick up the body" at the funeral home for a jazz funeral. Every band had regular members back then, some playing in more than one, but generally a regular lineup. Often those combinations gave each band a unique sound, so even if you did not see them coming, you could hear them from blocks away and identify them. Herman Sherman and Doc Watson were like Harold Dejan and Emanuel Paul; they were in perfect harmony and knew exactly where it was going without any communications. While you can't hear it in this picture, I think you can see it.
Near Poland and Alvar, 1985

Transcendental Payton

Walter Payton was a philosopher, an intellectual, and a black belt in karate. When he started playing one of his solos, he would take his audience on a voyage into another plane of existence and all other thoughts would evaporate. I knew him for over forty-five years and we always had fascinating conversations. His smile was contagious and he never sought the limelight but was perfectly content to remain in the penumbra of contemplation. The last time I saw Reginald Koeller was at the Satchmo Festival when he was playing with Walter Payton, Lucien Barbarin, and Dr. Michael White. As Walter wove his mystical magic on the bass, Reginald seemed to be transfixed, as was everyone onstage. Not long after this photo was taken, we lost "Reggie" and his very mellow sound and presence.
Satchmo Fest, Mint, circa 2003

Aw, Play That Thing

Pete Fountain was a legend in his own time. His Mardi Gras Day "Half-Fast Walking Club" became an intrinsic fixture in the "order of battle" for the day. The Jefferson City Buzzards sometimes preceded Pete, sometimes followed. It never mattered as long as both of them set the stage for Zulu, Rex, and Elks, who came later. Pete was a great inspiration to New Orleanians. He had "made it big" with Lawrence Welk in 1956 and I can still remember everyone in our family going down to Grandpa's to huddle around the only TV in the house to cheer him on. I first saw Pete playing with the Assuntos on the Horace Heidt radio show from the Municipal Auditorium and that was my very first live jazz concert. The little guy would come out in a bellhop uniform and say in this robot-like voice, "All aboard for Philip Morris," and the dancing cigarette packs would come out at the same time. We had a Zenith radio so I would spend many hours trying to play "Uncle Sheik's silver trumpet" while listening to Pete, the Assuntos, Tony Almerico, and all the others who were on WWL back then. I think one reason Pete was so respected and loved is that he never let his fame go to his head. He remained "just a New Orleans dude" who had this glorious "gift," as he always called it. Pete did not read music. He told me that when he went up to Welk's Orchestra, which was run like a symphony with every note on the chart, they had a hard time because he would just "take it and go." Either way it sure worked. It was a great tribute to see the outpouring of grief and love for Pete at his jazz funeral and also to see the "Half-Fast Walking Club" come waltzing, stumbling, and second lining down Bourbon on Mardi Gras Day.
Canal Street, circa 1984

A Star Is Born

It all started at Luigi's. Everyone reportedly was a little "elevated" that day when someone said, "Let's buy Wesley Schmidt a saxophone for his birthday." So a few of Luigi's regulars raided a local pawn shop to get Wesley a saxophone. The next logical step was to start a band. The only problem was that very few of the group knew how to play and certainly could not read music. So once they all had instruments a "pow wow" was arranged at Wesley's place on St. Anthony Avenue and the first steps toward bedlam were taken. I don't know how I got invited but someone either called on the phone or told me to come, so I showed up with my Yamaha student horn someone had given me rather than let it rust in the attic. I had taken lessons at both St. Aloysius with Professor Taverna in seventh through ninth grades and then with George Jansen and Frank Trippani at Loyola during high school, so I knew very little about jazz. Fortunately, a few who had played in high school showed up and that was a big help. Even though I had not played in many years, I took out the horn and said, "OK, everyone play this note!" A whirling dervish of cataclysmic, earsplitting sounds followed. "Now this one!" There came another Charles Ives, Frank Zappa, and Spike Jones trainwreck of sounds . . . and finally, "This one!" So there we had it, three notes that added up to F, A, and C. Next we did the change and went to C, E, and G. So now that we had it "up, down, sideways, and backwards," I said, "OK, let's go!" Everyone was surprised because this was obviously "inciting a riot," and of course everyone from Luigi's was always in the mood for that. Only one objection was made: "But we only know one song." I explained that since we would be marching no one would ever hear us twice. That taken care of, the entire "orchestra" literally tumbled out onto the front lawn and started marching down the neutral ground playing a "punk jazz classical calypso" version of "Joe Avery's Blues." From those first steps out onto the driveway, we see Woody Penouilh playing his first instrument, a wooden box drum. Few realized that the Tumblers, MOMS, Storyville Stompers, and Gentilly brass bands would all evolve from that very first "one-song parade." One day Woody rescued a tuba that was about to become a planter, and Tuba Fats told him, "If you learn to play that, you can get a lot of work." Woody rapidly rose in ability and stature and is now one of the best players in town. After Katrina, Woody was the *only* tuba player in town! All New Orleans jazz comes from the neighborhoods, which is exactly what happened with Woody. That was why "bringing them home" led to my first efforts the morning after Katrina's winds died down. That too grew into something international—the Arabi Wrecking Krewe, which wrecked Wesley's parents' house on Clermont Drive—and even financed a house for Al Carnival Johnson in Musicians' Village. In New Orleans, all it takes is a spark!
St. Anthony Avenue, 6000 block, 1979

"When the Tumblers began, I was afraid that my friends in the Olympia Brass Band would think that we were making fun of their music because we were so bad. At that time, Olympia was one of few bands that were still playing in the traditional New Orleans brass-band style. They were synonymous with this music. If you thought of New Orleans brass-band music back then, you would automatically picture their grand marshal, Richard 'the King' Matthews.

The Pair-O-Dice Tumblers were not trying to satirize Olympia's music or their efforts to preserve the brass-band culture. That was never the idea. We were having fun. And we were just bad at making music."

—Wesley Schmidt, grand marshal, Storyville Stompers

Blue-Eyed Soul

Here are two of my all-time favorite guys, Duane Yates and Harry Ravain. Duane was the best "blue-eyed soul" singer I ever heard. He gave 100 percent with every song and was often completely exhausted at the end of a set. I knew Harry from high-school days. He always wanted to play with the Boogie Kings and when he finally got that chance, a coronary almost ended his life. When I went to the hospital to see him, all he could say was, "Man, I got to get out of here and get back to the band!" Well, fortunately, Harry did get his chance to play with them. One Mardi Gras, I was putting a band together to play for WDSU on Mardi Gras Day and we needed a drummer. Harry was already booked so he said, "Look, I got a guy. He's a bit on the funky side musically, but he's fantastic." Well, that dude turned out to be the great Freddie Staehle of Dr. John fame. I never saw a drummer who could play four rhythms at once, but Freddie did it that day. Even before the broadcast he wanted to warm up, and as he started playing, just a half-block from Gallier Hall, the entire crowd quieted so they could hear him. The man was a genius. We did so well with him leading us that, when we broke into "Watermelon Man," the control room cut away from the announcers and we went out over a worldwide HDTV network for seventeen minutes uninterrupted. Both Harry and Duane are now playing up in some really rocking place, of that I am certain. They are sadly missed and forever remembered.
Musicians' Alumni Association Concert, Downtown, 1996

New Orleans Style

Impeccably dressed and on time, Mr. Teddy Johnson knows his instrument and enjoys playing with others. The secret to New Orleans music is in the listening and "fitting in" with the other players. It's not playing the loudest, the highest, or the fastest; it's the ensemble playing with a melody that's coherent. Herman Sherman told me, "Find a spot where there's no music and put some in there."
Jackson Square, 1975

It All Started Here

Leroy Jones got his musical start in a school band. Two years later he joined the Fairview Baptist Church Christian Marching Band, where he got his start in New Orleans brass-band music. The church was originally located on St. Denis Street, very close to Leroy's home. When Danny introduced me to Leroy, I realized instantly that this was someone headed for greatness. Leroy could warm up better than almost anyone could play. Plus, he was a serious musician who took great care in learning his craft, improving his ability, and making it his lifetime career. He, like so many others, got his start with Danny Barker and the Fairview Baptist Church band. Since then he's been with Harry Connick, Jr., and virtually all the brass bands. He had his own Hurricane Brass Band, and after that, Leroy Jones & New Orleans' Finest have played all over the world, creating his own style and sound.
St. Bernard Avenue, 1976

"Now if we want to speak about beginnings, this photo tells that story on me. It must be circa mid-1970s? I'm posing, with trumpet pointed heavenward, out in front of the original Fairview Baptist Church. The church used to be located at the corner of Buchanan and St. Denis streets, perhaps only sixty meters from my boyhood home in the Seventh Ward neighborhood where I grew up and had my formal training in music. It was here where I met Pastor Andrew Darby, Sr., and many of his church members. One particular member of the church's congregation was famous jazz guitarist/historian Danny Barker, who was also my neighbor, residing just around the corner from the church, on Sere Street. Well, when Reverend Darby asked Mr. Barker to find some youngsters who played instruments suitable for the youth band he envisioned, I was among the first recruits. At the time there weren't enough young musicians attending Fairview who played instruments suitable to complete the type of band being established, a brass band. That band became known as the Fairview Baptist Church Christian Marching Band, later to be known simply as the Fairview Band. Through my meeting Danny Barker and being a part of this history-making aggregation, I developed an early understanding of and appreciation for a tradition that's been carried on in the city of New Orleans for over a century."

—Leroy Jones

Jack Willis and Teddy Riley

If one wants to know what a New Orleans brass-band musician should look and sound like, here are two perfect examples. Jack was Ray Charles' first trumpet player for nineteen years. When I met him, he was in the later years of his career and played a mellophone instead of trumpet. I told Gregg Stafford that Jack did not seem to smile a lot and Gregg laughed and said, "That's because he had a stroke." Stroke or not, Jack could play that horn beautifully and I started emulating his "parts" in my own playing. Both Jack and Teddy played with Young Tuxedo and Onward. Teddy had his own Royal Brass Band as well. At Teddy's funeral, one of his original neighbors said, "When Teddy started playing that trumpet, everyone closed their windows he was so bad." By persistence and talent, Teddy came to be known as "the guy who can play anything in any key." When these two were coming up in the music world, it was necessary to be able to read music, and transpose into any key. They also took great pride in their appearance and were always on time. They did not drink on the job and played their best at all times. I had a chance to play with both of them on occasion, and like Leroy Jones and Satchmo, they made you sound good!
Ninth Ward, 1985

Like Father, Like Son

Here we see Walter and Nicholas Payton at Tulane with the Young Tuxedo Brass Band. I knew Walter since the '60s and used to see him out on the Claiborne Avenue neutral ground practicing his karate. It's such a delight to see his son not only following in his footsteps but making a huge career playing his own way, in his own style. I made Nicholas's set recently in the Jazz Fest Jazz Tent and it was amazing! Nicholas shares his father's philosophical nature, and his music is original and creative.
Tulane University, circa 1978

Barney Floyd

A Gary, Indiana, native who graduated from Western Michigan University, Barney played for ten years with the Ringling Brothers, Shrine, and other circus bands before winding up in New Orleans. He would come here every year as the circus made its rounds and met a local singer, Elizabeth Messina, in 1999. Barney plays in Broadway shows, casinos, and big bands, does studio sessions, and is very well known for his incredible range and professionalism. He has four Grammy nominations for appearing on albums, winning two of the awards. He's been playing the Commander's Palace brunch for years and has twin daughters who were born in 2005. Barney lost two houses that year, as he had just moved to St. Bernard and his old Uptown double flooded as well. Even so, he was one of the staunchest supporters of and participants in the Arabi Wrecking Krewe in the months and years that followed.
Royal Street, 2014

Kenneth Terry

I first met Kenny at a Treme Brass Band gig. We played together at Ernie K-Doe's funeral and I have been following his career ever since. Always a great showman, he puts on a great performance with the trumpet or the microphone.
French Quarter Fest Jazz Stage, 2010

Lillian Boutte

I first met Lillian in Ascona in 2006. I always knew of her but she had been living in Germany, so I never had the chance to meet her before then. We hit it off instantly because of my work with both the Arabi Wrecking Krewe and the photography support I had been giving to New Orleans Musicians' Clinic before then. Lillian is not only a great singer; she is a humanitarian who was not reluctant to stand up for New Orleans. After Katrina, she was touring in Europe and raising thousands of dollars at every performance for the Arabi Wrecking Krewe, of which she became a founding board member. We toured Italy, Germany, and Switzerland, raising awareness of the true situation concerning the manmade flood of 2005. We appeared together along with Dr. Michael White in *The Sound After the Storm,* which won first prize at the Zurich Film Festival. There are not enough words to describe the charisma and talent that Lillian possesses. Her indomitable spirit was instrumental in keeping the Wrecking Krewe going through the darkest of times.

Brian O'Neill

Brian was both a trombonist and an arranger. His death in 2005 on the heels of Katrina was a huge blow to the music community, since Brian was a universally liked and respected musician. His jazz funeral was one of the most emotional ever seen in New Orleans.
Jazz Fest, 2003

Tell It Like It Is

Eddie Bocage, best known as Eddie Bo, had several really big hits. Eddie was a carpenter by trade, but he could make those keys fly. He told me that when he was first starting out, he was such a perfectionist that his hands would bleed from the hours of pounding. He said that one day he was talking to Professor Longhair, who told him, "Just play, man. You got it." And once Eddie did that, it all fell into place.
Ascona Jazz Festival, 2008

Detroit Brooks

Detroit plays banjo and guitar with equal virtuosity. He wrote one of the best songs about Katrina; I hope he recorded it! Like everyone else in Gentilly, he had ten feet of water in his house. The Arabi Wrecking Krewe got it ready for rebuilding. Detroit is one of those guys who just avoids the spotlight but plays with a perfection that is hard to miss. His brother, Mark, is one of the premier bass players in the world.
Ascona Jazz Festival, 2008

David and Popee

Here are two of the famous Lastie family, David on sax and Walter on drums. Their brother Melvin is credited with the first trumpet solo on an R&B record, "I Know." David was so free of ego that when you played with him, he would say, "Thanks for letting me play." His was a true New Orleans sound. Popee played the drum introduction for Eddie Bo's hit record "Tell It Like It Is." They were two really great New Orleanians. I worked with their sister, Betty, at the Music Street Food Stamp Office and she was a great gospel singer as well.
Royal Street, 1980

David Paquette

David was born in Connecticut, but his family made frequent trips to New Orleans and were among the first to attend Preservation Hall concerts. So at a very early age, David was introduced to New Orleans jazz. He transferred to LSU and it was not long before he found Pat O'Brien's, with its famous twin-piano bar. His credits are a mile long. He was director of the Waiheke Festival in New Zealand for seventeen years, started the Paquette Jazz Foundation, and still plays all over the world. David's hands are so fast that when he does his trademark "lowest key and highest key simultaneously" move, it might take hundreds of tries to catch it in a photo. He is a great entertainer who relates to his audience and can play just about anything. Ask him about the feathers in front his door every morning in Ascona!
Ascona, 2017

Paddy Sherlock

While Paddy has never been to New Orleans, I can honestly say he is going to take the town by storm. I met him in Ascona and never laughed so hard in all my life. As a trombonist he's world class, but I suspect there is a grand marshal hiding inside that mischievous smile. His antics with Ellen Birath are as close to those of Louis Prima and Keely Smith as anyone I have ever seen. I hope he's here for St. Patrick's Day because I know it will make both my Irish grandmothers smile. Get ready, New Orleans, Hurricane Paddy is headed our way!
Ascona, 2017

"Why do I want to come to New Orleans? Because when I was a kid I played classical piano like a good south-side Dublin middle-class kid should. And I was apparently very good but I hated it and wanted to give up. But at the same time I was completely immersed in music. I listened and sang all day.

Luckily, I had a zany uncle who understood the kid. He gave me a trombone and a record, *George Brunis King of the Tailgate Trombone.* I started copying him. The first song I ever learned was 'Tin Roof Blues.' The next album I got was Sweet Emma and the Preservation Hall Band. I learned big Jim Robinson's solo off 'Ice Cream.' Here's me, this Dublin suburbs kid, playing along with the best of them. I didn't know it was jazz. It was just music to me. And I've always been that way. I don't differentiate jazz from other music. It's all just good music (if it's good . . .). Anyway, next was Armstrong. Then Ella, then Louis Jordan, and all the time Kid Ory, and then the marching bands. So I was thrown into the melting pot of mainly New Orleans music from the youngest age and it has always been a huge part of my music. When I was young I used to say, 'I'll go to New Orleans next year.' And I've been all over the world but not to New Orleans yet. . . . It slipped out of my hands. Now I really want to go. Hanging out in Ascona with so many heads from New Orleans has re-whetted my appetite. It's time to do my musical Hajj—bring my T-bone and bring my songwriting and see what I can't absorb, assimilate, and also bring to New Orleans. I'm coming home soon."

—Paddy Sherlock, Dublin, Ireland

Glen David

Glen David Andrews is from Treme in New Orleans. He got started on trombone at the urging of his cousin, "Trombone Shorty," and first played with Shorty's brother, James Andrews. Glen played with the Little Rascals, Rebirth, and Dirty Dozen and then spent a few years perfecting his style playing with Tuba Fats in Jackson Square. His thundering trombone volleys can be heard for blocks and his singing is right out of the gospel/soul/traditional jazz genres. Glen has had his share of obstacles but he's turned his life around, and if you ever hear him sing "We Shall Overcome," you will get the feeling that we surely will. He is a giant in the New Orleans music scene and one of the city's most popular musicians everywhere he goes.
Ascona, 2017

I Got Time on My Hands

Uncle Lionel always wore his watch on his left hand. When asked about it, he would always say, "I got time on my hands." This was one of his trademarks, of which there were many.
Ascona, 2007

Chapter 7

Second Lines

Who Dat?

The second line is one of the most universal of all New Orleans dance forms. It's unrehearsed, spontaneous, and anyone can do it. A wonderful song, "The Second Line," by Paul Barbarin, really tells the story: "When you hear that beat, New Orleans you will greet." It is generally done with an umbrella, white rag, napkin, hat, pipe wrench, whiskey bottle, or anything you can get your hands on. The world over, the second line says one thing: "New Orleans." Sometimes its tens of thousands, other times it's just one person, but it's always just moments from happening. Let the Saints win a game, or a band come passing by, and there it is. When I lived on First Street, one block from St. Charles Avenue, I used to hear the social and pleasure clubs having their second lines on Sundays. Follow the sound and sure enough the celebration is on. This one was in Treme on a hot summer day.
Treme, 1985

BMOL on Parade

The Black Men of Labor is a benevolent society based in Treme. Fred Johnson, Jr., Benny Jones, Sr., and Gregory Stafford founded the organization in 1993. The mission of the BMOL is to "reaffirm and pay tribute to the contributions of African American men in the work place while promoting and preserving Traditional Jazz Music." The BMOL celebrates its West African and Caribbean culture and traditions in the Treme and around the world with authentic African outfits and dancing to traditional jazz music. That includes Cuba Son and Conga Line, Haiti Ra Ra, and Dominican Republic Ga-Ga Dancing. Their second lines are among the most colorful of all those held in New Orleans.
St. Claude Avenue, 2015

Blue Tarp Bendovah!

The Tucks Marching Club never fails to dazzle, amaze, shock, or amuse onlookers with their often outrageous themes and costuming. Two years after Katrina, they featured the "Bendovah Construction Krewe" motif to "honor" the contractors who descended on New Orleans after the flood and became infamous for taking deposits and never doing any work. The highlight of the Bendovah's costumes was a large stainless-steel screw glued on top of their helmets. The krewe sashayed down Napoleon and St. Charles to Gallier Hall, where they gave a fitting salute to our mayor.
St. Charles Avenue, 2007

All You Need Is a Napkin

Here we see Brant Schmidt, DDS, demonstrating perfect form and technique with the "left-handed napkin pirouette." His sister, Audrey, is the bride and the occasion is, of course, her wedding reception. She has opted for the more classical "umbrella arabesque."
Metry, 2001

Two Second Liners

Eddie Fusch and Gregg Stafford prepare for the BMOL second line on St. Claude Avenue. As one can readily see, attire varies for the occasion, but like most things in New Orleans, everything is both negotiable and acceptable. To a Yat (of which I am proudly one!), the white socks are required and suitable for any black-tie occasion.
Sweet Lorraine's, 2013

Turnaround

When the hats turn around, you know it's *on* and that it's going to be a great afternoon. Since almost everything in New Orleans is spontaneous, one can never predict what's going to happen next. On this particular afternoon, Henry Dudley was leading the Onward band through intermittent rain as we headed down Orleans toward the Quarter. When the rain stopped, spirits lifted and things got really hot, both from the steam off the street and the rhythm of the drums. Gregg Stafford on bass drum with Freddie Kohlman on snare were an "unbeatable" combination that day. We wound up at Johnny White's drinking "medicine" with Lawrence Trotter, Herman Sherman, Jack Willis, Kid Sheik, and Henry Dudley. The last thing I remember is Gregg helping me up off the floor!
Orleans Avenue, 1994

Never Too Young

There are no rigid guidelines to second-line accessories. The smallest umbrella, the largest one . . . it matters not.
St. Claude Avenue, 2011

Saints 31 Colts 17

I pick this caption because it perfectly captures the elation that swept over this city on that day and night. There were no broken windows or burned cars, but there was a "riot" on Bourbon Street that night that spread throughout the entire region. After forty-three years of disappointment, New Orleans *finally* got its Super Bowl win. There was a lot of criticism for Peyton Manning in other places. Some were saying, "He threw the game since he was from New Orleans." Well, actually he sorta did. You see, Peyton always wanted to play with the Saints in the Super Bowl and to throw the winning pass, and actually he *did!* I wrote to the Indianapolis newspaper and said, "If you don't want him, we'll take him back!" Anyone in New Orleans that weekend will never forget what it was like. The older citizens said, "It was just like VE Day." It may never happen again, but we had our day!
Bourbon Street, 2010

Treme Second Line

This is how it's supposed to be.
Treme, 2010

I Wanna Do That When I Grow Up!

Every young child in New Orleans is exposed to second lines and jazz almost from birth. It really starts there and it carries forward for life. The awe in the little boys' eyes is obvious.
Central City, 2000

Chapter 8

Jazz Funerals

Anthony "Tuba Fats"

I knew "Fats" ever since Gregg Stafford introduced me to him in 1973. Anthony was the "gentle giant" who would often help the Grand Marshal by spinning his tuba like a feather to cut through the crowd. Whenever I met anyone anywhere in the world who was coming to visit New Orleans, I would tell them, "Just go to Jackson Square and look for the big guy playing the tuba. He'll show you where to go." I would find Anthony out there at all hours sitting on an iron bench, usually surrounded by other musicians who just wanted to play. One day I hope to get a statue of him put on that bench to remind people what a real musician looks like. His jazz funeral was the biggest I have ever seen. At least fifty tubas were in that giant band, and tens of thousands lined the route. I sure do miss him.
Preservation Hall gate, 2004

Uncle Lionel

It is a New Orleans tradition to hold a wake the night before a funeral. When Frog Joseph's wake was held the night before his jazz funeral, music was the centerpiece of the night. Uncle Lionel sang "I'll Fly Away," his signature song, and as always, he gave the perfect performance for the occasion and healed hearts sad with grief.
Tharp Funeral Home, 2004

Gathering of the Band

The traditional jazz funeral starts at a local "watering hole" near the funeral home from which the deceased is taken to the services. This gathering of the band is more a coming together than a "pre-party." This is a very important distinction that "newbies" have to understand. It *is* a funeral, not a party or photo op. It's a *real* funeral.
Seal's Class Act, St. Bernard Avenue, 2004

Baby Dolls

This is another longstanding New Orleans tradition. Originating in Storyville, the "ladies of the evening" would "sashay through the streets" on Mardi Gras morning to get more "business." Officially chartered in 1925, the Baby Dolls now have a very different meaning. With their brightly colored satin dresses and ornate umbrellas, they add elegance and style to any second line, parade, or jazz funeral they attend.
Corpus Christi Church, St. Bernard Avenue, 2015

Slow Drag

Black Men of Labor do the "slow drag" as they lead a funeral procession. Note that the crowd is *not* intruding into the space for the first line, which is the Grand Marshal, the band, and the family.
Treme, 2004

Herman Sherman's Service

Once the procession has reached the church, the mood remains somber and the band continues playing nothing but dirges. Fortunately, Herman made sure that the leadership of the Young Tuxedo Jazz Band was passed on to Gregg Stafford, who has kept it traditional in every sense of the word. Catch them at Jazz Fest to hear the *real* music.
St. Rose Church, 1984

Half-Fast Walking Club Banners

On the occasion of Pete Fountain's jazz funeral, his famous walking club showed up with all of the banners from his decades of leading the merry band on Mardi Gras Day. I first saw them in the '60s, when they were dressed like Roman legionnaires, rollicking down Royal Street.
Jackson Square, 2016

Blow Down the Sky!

Before every jazz funeral, you will hear someone say to the assembled band, "Blow down the sky!" The first time I ever heard it was from Mrs. Lawrence Trotter, before the funeral for Charles Barbarin, Sr.
Pete Fountain's funeral, Royal Street, 2016

Mitch Landrieu

I had the distinct honor of working in City Hall when "Moon" Landrieu was mayor. His saying of "Pride Builds New Orleans" rang true then and especially after Katrina. Moon saved the Superdome from being just another $200 million hole in the ground like the World's Fair. As mayor, his son, Mitch, revitalized the city and made inroads into getting us back to being the "Paris of America." Mitch made me feel pride in my hometown, and we're lucky to have had him to bring us along as far as he could from the disaster of Katrina. Here he is second lining at Pete Fountain's jazz funeral.

Royal Street, 2016

Pete

Royal Street, 2016

Frog's Trombone

This was the first time I ever saw it not in his hands. Frog was a magician. My father knew him back in the '40s and '50s, and we used to go up on Esplanade at Claiborne where the "People's Policies Pay Promptly" Funeral Home was located. We'd stand on the neutral ground under the majestic oaks that lined Claiborne and watch the processions form up and "kick off." Fortunately for the world, Frog left us Gerald, Kirk, and Charles, all world-class musicians whom I consider family.
Steps of Corpus Christi, 2004

Kirk Joseph

Kirk, Gerald, and Charles led the procession for their father, Waldren "Frog" Joseph, out of Corpus Christi. Kirk was wearing a "frog tie" and "blowing down the sky." The photograph being carried in the procession is one I shot of Kirk's father, Frog, in 1975.
Steps of Corpus Christi Church, 2004

Pallbearers

At times it's heartbreaking to shoot photos. Sometimes I just won't do it if I think it's too invasive or disrespectful. However, Lillian Boutte asked me to photograph her mother's funeral and I did as she asked. I had known Ms. Gloria since Katrina, when Lillian joined forces with me and others to form the organization that came to be known as the "Arabi Wrecking Krewe." As the band plays a dirge, the pallbearers take the coffin to the hearse, where it will be transported to the cemetery. The crowd stays a respectful distance away and honors the memory of the deceased.
Corpus Christi Church, 2015

K-Doe's Last Ride

Ernie K-Doe was one of the all-time greatest characters to ever live in New Orleans. His jazz funeral was one of the biggest ever held and it lasted for hours. K-Doe had so many number-one hits that he became the self-proclaimed "Emperor of the Universe," and no one doubted that for a minute. When I was fifteen and just starting to play guitar, we wound up "backing" him for his big hit "Wanted—$10,000 Reward." When we asked him what key to play it in, he said, "Any key." The man was a musical genius! His show on WWOZ was a classic.
Canal Street at Rampart, 2001

Burn, K-Doe, Burn!

Ernie was truly the "Emperor of the Universe," as he proudly proclaimed every time he got on that WWOZ microphone. His record of hits in the early '60s was unparalleled. His funeral was so large it tied up the CBD for two hours. His legacy still burns brightly today.
Claiborne at Canal, 2001

Jazz Funeral, Uptown

This is the first jazz funeral I photographed. It started on Oak Street and wound its way to the cemetery by the "Priest Factory" on Carrollton Avenue. This is how a jazz funeral should look: first line in the street, second line on the sidewalk. This way everyone gets to hear the music, do their second-line thing, and get their pictures without disgracing the occasion.
A few blocks from Carrollton Avenue, 1972

Lead On!

A funeral procession turns off Oak Street on the way to the cemetery. Olympia was the band that day. *Oak Street, 1975*

Reflections

Dr. Michael White is visible in this reflection on the side of the hearse. *Location and date unknown*

Salute and Farewell

Pork Chop stands by as the hearse with Henry Dudley in it is "cut loose" to go to the cemetery. Pork Chop is wearing Henry's tuxedo, top hat, and sash in what he told me was his very first time being a Grand Marshal. The moment the "body is cut loose," the handkerchief is removed from the snare drum, the signal that the celebration begins. That's the proper way to do it.
Basin Street, 2004

Pork Chop Lost in Treme

It was understandable, since this was his first time being a Grand Marshal. Pork Chop was leading the second line after the departure of the hearse so he headed for the nearest bar. The only problem was everyone else headed for a different one. So I had to run after Pork Chop and finally got him to turn around and get back in front the band.
Somewhere in Treme, 2004

Rico and Jones

This story begins in 1979 during the police strike at Mardi Gras. The mayor had threatened arrest of anyone who ventured out, and of course, the Pair-O-Dice Tumblers just had to defy that order. After a short confrontation with some police cadets at Esplanade and Decatur, our wild band moved down its traditional route to the Cathedral. When we finally got to the front of the church, suddenly these shrill trumpet notes came flying over the din that the Tumblers called "Marching Music Therapy." This crazy guy was standing on top of a fire hydrant, blowing down the sky as if he was Gabriel himself. Being quick to recognize talent, the Tumblers incorporated this new addition into the Tumble. I got to know "Rico" (aka Larry Talerico in "real" life) and still do today. In this picture, he's playing with Benny Jones at the funeral for Ms. Gloria Boutte.
Corpus Christi Church, 2015

"While on sabbatical from teaching, I came to New Orleans the year of the police strike somewhere around Mardi Gras . . . and *stayed!* I played my first Mardi Gras with the Tumblers and said, '*Wow* . . . this is *it!* . . . Such enthusiasm and spirit.' I then started the Storyville Stompers, a really fun soulful brass band, in 1980. Currently, I am performing with three different bands in addition to my own jazz trio, the Levee Jazz Trio. Since coming to New Orleans, I have been strongly influenced by Milton Batiste, the Original Olympia Brass Band, Leroy Jones, and Jeremy Davenport. I don't ever plan on moving away, because the music, food, architecture, and wonderful people are unlike any I have ever found in any other part of the world."

—Larry Talerico, musician, retired manager of Latter and Blum Uptown office

Reality

Everyone must always remember that for all the second-line antics, a jazz funeral is a real funeral. There is plenty of room in the tradition to dance, sing, play, and celebrate the liberation of the deceased. There is also decorum, lines that are not crossed, things that are not done. Every newcomer to the city should take the time to find out what our traditions are and help us to observe and preserve them. Coming here from somewhere else and trying to change our way of doing things is to destroy the very reason you came here in the first place.
Jackson Avenue Cemetery, 2005

Didn't He Ramble

Once the burial is completed, the handkerchief is removed from the snare, the umbrellas open, the hats get turned around, and the celebration begins.
St. Louis Cemetery by City Park, 2004

Saints Go Marchin' In!

I wanna be in *that* number!
St. Louis Cemetery by City Park, 2004

I Be's Tired, but My Soul Is at Rest

Wet, tired, blown out, but content that a proper send-off has been given to one of our own. Woody Penouilh and Larry Talerico after Gloria Boutte's funeral.
St. Bernard Avenue, 2015

Paparazzi

Johnny Donnels told me in the '80s that he had stopped shooting jazz funerals because of the behavior of both the crowd and the photographers. An attitude now exists that the funeral is nothing more than a party or a chance to "cash in" by selling pictures of the event. There is nothing wrong with shooting photos of the funeral; there is everything wrong with pushing, shoving, coming into the band, and hitting instruments. I started a Facebook page called "Ethical Jazz Photographers" to try to educate all these self-proclaimed "artists" who treat the tradition as a steppingstone for their "careers." All of the images I have captured over a fifty-year period have never come at the expense or embarrassment of the musicians, second liners, or families. A good idea is to try to devote a percentage of the profits from photo sales to either the persons depicted or something like the Musicians' Clinic. Mostly just get your shot and *move!* If this trend continues, there won't be any more jazz funerals. It's that simple.
Jackson Square in front of St. Louis Cathedral, 2015

For Whom the Drum Tolls

This completes a voyage into the jazz funeral tradition, its origins, meanings, and purpose. Anyone who has read this book now knows the real tradition and hopefully will act accordingly. Hitting a wind-instrument player's horn can ruin a career and further destroy our traditions. I sure hope at least a few will use this knowledge and help preserve what makes the "City That Care Forgot" live on.
The Young Tuxedo bass drum, over one hundred years old, 2005

Chapter 9

FRENCH QUARTER

St. Louis Cathedral

This landmark is known the world over as the center of Jackson Square and of the Catholic tradition in New Orleans. Built in 1718, it is the oldest cathedral in the United States. It was raised to basilica status in 1793 and rebuilt to the current appearance in 1850. In 1987, Pope John Paul II visited the church, and a bronze plaque commemorating the event can be seen directly in front. In typical New Orleans fashion, it is said that the ghost of Pere Antoine, a priest buried in the church, walks the alley on the downriver side of the building that is named in his honor. The support columns inside are slightly tilted inward to support the weight of the ceiling, so be sure to look for that when you are there.
Jackson Square, spring of 1986

Bourbon Street at Night

This is another world-famous New Orleans landmark. Virtually no one comes to the city without at least a quick peek at our naughtiest street. Back in the '50s and early '60s, the Desire streetcar traveled right down the middle but was unfortunately removed, taking away one of the best streetcar rides in the world! No visit to the Crescent City would be complete without at least a walk down this neon-lit, cacophonous thoroughfare.
Sugar Bowl night 1985 from the balcony of the Royal Sonesta looking downriver

Pere Antoine Alley at midnight

The ghost of Pere Antoine is said to walk this alley late at night. You might take a ghost tour to see all the haunted places in the French Quarter, or better yet, Halloween in New Orleans has become as much of an event as Mardi Gras Eve. In either case, be ready for a thrill when walking down this alley at 3:00 AM with your third Hurricane in your hand.
Pere Antoine Alley facing north, 1983

Lucky Dog Stand

New Orleans is world-famous for its nearly unlimited range of restaurants, po'-boy shops, gumbo shops, and any imaginable style of food from anywhere in the world. For some, the Lucky Dog is a great delicacy. You won't have any trouble finding one on Bourbon Street in the afternoon or at night. I prefer Yo Mama's, next to Johnny White's, for their hamburger or the Gumbo Shop for that genuine okra seafood gumbo. To each his own . . . and in New Orleans, you have to search long and hard for a bad restaurant.
Royal Sonesta, 2016

Bar at Yo Mama's

My two hangouts in the Quarter are side by side, Johnny White's and Yo Mama's. There are as many bars as churches in New Orleans, so no one can't find a watering hole to call their own. Many a night I have been in those two places with the musicians from Preservation Hall coming in to catch a quick beer between sets. Yo Mama's has the best burger and baked potato in town!
St. Peter Street across from Preservation Hall, 1996

Bourbon Street during Police Strike of 1979

Freezing-cold rain pours down, with not a policeman to be found anywhere in the city . . . except for Deputy Chief Chuck Ladell and a handful others. It was a first for New Orleanians, since we never had a police strike before or since. I was out there on the picket line carrying the badges, guns, and radios for several cops I knew. There was a very strange feeling around town, which I think the picture captures. All ended well, though. Crime actually went *down* during the strike, and for those who ventured out into the Quarter that Mardi Gras Day, the experience was only equaled by the first post-Katrina Mardi Gras in 2006. Behind the camera is the site of the old French Opera House. Built in 1857, it burned down in 1919 and was never rebuilt.

Bourbon Street facing the river, 1979

Fountain at Pat O'Brien's

One of the rites of passage in New Orleans was always to go to Pat O's for your first bar visit when you made eighteen. The patio has this great fountain with a fire in the middle. For some reason, every time I went down there with my pals from St. Aloysius or Cor Jesu (and later on UNO, Loyola, USL, LSU, Southern, UNO again, Tulane Grad School, or Delgado), we always wound up around that fountain singing "When the Saints Go Marchin' In." The reason there is a fence around the fountain today is no doubt because often we wound up standing in it at the end of the night! It's still there, as are the two great pianos inside the piano bar. So be sure to have at least two Hurricanes before you decide to call it a night!

Pat O'Brien's, 2016

Faulkner House

William Faulkner did live here and surely got some of his ideas from doing exactly what everyone does at least some of the time in New Orleans, "hanging out in da Quarter." That alley is Pirate's Alley, and there is quite a story about Jean Lafitte negotiating with Gen. Andrew Jackson there to spy on the British before the Battle of New Orleans down in Chalmette.

Back of St. Louis Cathedral looking toward Canal Street, 1985

Moonrise over the Courthouse

Rick Trolsen wrote a song called "Sunrise on Bourbon Street" that captures what happens when you stay out all night in the Quarter and suddenly realize that the sun has come up, and you can't remember the last four or five hours. That's not what happened to get this picture, but let's say it has happened a "few" times in my voyages into the twilight zone of New Orleans. Read Frenchy Brouillette's book, *Mr. New Orleans,* to get the whole story!
St. Peter, looking at the moon on the way to the Moonwalk, 2003

Jeanne d'Arc statue

We got so much from the French in the time they owned Louisiana. French bread, French Quarter, French wine, Cajun French, Cajuns, Ragin' Cajuns, Frenchmen Street . . . you get the picture. This beautiful statue resides on a little triangle of land just before Decatur meets up with Ursuline Avenue. You may have noticed we never use addresses in New Orleans. It's always, "You know, back by that old bank building near Monahan's Irish bar where all the second lines start in the Quarter." This is a great statue and I hope you get a chance to see it on your way to Central Grocery to get your muffuletta!
Decatur at Ursuline, 2016

Fire Watch

In New Orleans, we have the most wonderful relationship with our firepersons. I think it's from the city burning down a few times, so we've come to revere these true heroes. After all, who wants to run into a burning building to save a stranger? These people do it without even thinking. Louie "the Nooge" Nugent was a fireman and the most diehard Saints fan who ever lived (in a tie with Francis Boudreaux). Man, he got me *ten* tickets to the Saints' first playoff game, which of course they blew. He was up there on the snorkel at the Cabildo fire, breathing that acrid air and putting out that fire. Capt. Raymond Spain was also a U.S. Marine and a fireman. I knew them both for over fifty years—good timers who loved New Orleans with a passion seldom seen anywhere else.

So whenever we see one of our firepersons, we know that while they seem to be lounging around a lot of the time, when that alarm rings, they are *all business!* They are great New Orleanians who never get enough credit for what they do. Be sure to wave at them when they go by or say, "Where *yat?*" They are the people who will pull you out of hell and save your life in a heartbeat.

St. Peter Street at Jackson Square, 2003

Flowers in the Quarter

It may not seem obvious, but if you walk down any street or into any business in the Quarter, you will see flowers everywhere.
Royal and St. Peter, 1994

Quarter Gargoyle

Even the statues in the French Quarter get into the Mardi Gras mood. This is one to search for; a clue is that it's on a street parallel to Canal, near the Royal Sonesta. Locals with a few years on them will remember the Morgus the Magnificent treasure hunts when he was on TV in the '50s. Rumor has it that Chopsley put those beads up there all those years ago.
X Street, 2017

Buster Holmes

If you only had a quarter, and were in the Quarter, Buster Holmes was the place to go for your red beans and rice. Buster was an amazing, kind, and generous New Orleanian. For two dollars back in the late '60s, you could get your red beans, cornbread, maybe a nice piece of chicken or pork chop, bread pudding, and a drink. Buster closed his soul-food restaurant in the early '80s and died in 1994. If there is a heaven, Buster is up there feeding everyone!
721 Burgundy. 2005

"I never went to New Orleans until I met my husband-to-b in Houston. He was born in Houston but his dad worked for the shipyards. His dad was transferred to New Orleans, so my husband grew up in New Orleans. He came from a family of four boys and four girls. I grew up with one brother. When we traveled to New Orleans, we went to see his family and friends. I met the majority of them at 'the family picnic.' Afterwards, we would go to the Quarter, listen to music, and when we got hungry, he would take me to a little hole-in-the-wall restaurant that had the best gumbo I have ever tasted. When it was time to go back to Houston, I would always cry. I had such a wonderful time, so much love. New Orleans is the City of Dreams, ya know."

—Sally Steubben, native of Houston, Texas

Chapter 10

New Orleans Characters

Francis Boudreaux

Francis was the consummate master auto mechanic and one of the greatest of all the Saints fans. Many a Friday I would be over at his shop on Clematis Street helping out both with drinking those six-packs and fixing the "dogs" (cars that just would not run) before the owners would come to pick them up. I used to wonder why he had so many junk VWs parked in his lot, until I started going over there on Fridays. Those were his free spare parts for the cars that belonged to people who were struggling to get by in life. I saw him do miracles with those heaps and turn them into Ferraris. If ever there was a kind, fair, honest, and decent mechanic and great New Orleanian, it was "Boud," as we all called him. "Coach" would often call me up just to make sure my VW was still going, and if it wasn't, he would soon be over with his tool bag to get it going again. When Boud had cancer, he would go directly from chemo to the Superdome to watch his beloved Saints. He made *every* game they ever played, until he was so ill he could no longer go. His greatest possession was the designer Saints watch that Buddy D gave him for his sign in the Dome during one of our 1 and 15 seasons! I think this photo captures his true spirit.

Balcony, Bourbon Street, 2004

Clermont Drive Wesley

Here's a character who can *only* exist in New Orleans. Wesley Schmidt lived a block up from my house on Clermont Drive. I've known him for as long as I can remember, from Union Playground. Wesley is one of our grandest of Grand Marshals and he has the suits to prove it! One in particular, the lavender one, caught my eye at the first Jazz Fest after Katrina, and I told him, "I wanna be buried in that one!" Wesley's comment in his best and always effervescent humor was, "You can, but you got to give it back!" He makes the best pineapple-juice drink in the world.
Jazz Fest, 2006

Gerhard "Doggy" Hund

Doggy led the Maryland Jazz Band, which came to New Orleans from its home base in Germany many times. Doggy was a great trombonist, educator, and friend. He always made sure his band played it exactly right and he did a lot to help us out after Katrina. Here he's with Don Vappie at the "Pay the Rent" party at Howlin' Wolf after bringing his band over to help raise funds for our culture bearers. Out of respect for Doggy, his band continues on and has changed its name to New Orleans Jazz Band to honor his memory.
Howlin' Wolf, 2006

Kelle Reichert

A former queen of Tucks and wife of its co-captain and founder Robert, Kelle stands here behind his float on parade Saturday 2017. We lost Bobby, but, as this photo demonstrates, we have not lost his spirit!
Napoleon Avenue at Magazine, 2017

Uncle Donald Ka'moi

One of the most amazing things I ever discovered was the connection between Hawai'i and Louisiana. On my first visit there, the Hawaiian band started playing a song I was *very* familiar with, "You Are My Sunshine." Later I was to discover that Jimmie Davis paid a Hawaiian for the music and added the words to what is now the official Louisiana state song. Uncle and I used to stay up all night making leis to sell to the tourists the next day at his hula show at the Maui Hilton. I made the mistake once of only using the purple and gold flowers, since the "Black Label" flowed freely that night. Fortunately, an entire busload of Ragin' Cajuns showed up at the show the next day and just *loved* the "LSU leis."
Maui, 1996

All Lives Matter

While driving down Magazine Street, I noticed this little guy sitting in a doorway in front of a house near Jackson Avenue. I shot this picture through the open window of my beat-up VW while sitting at the red light, and I always wondered what happened to that child. I did not notice, in that short moment before the light changed and I had to drive off, that he did not have any shoes on. If I had noticed, I would have bought him a pair of nice tennis shoes. Since that day, I am always on the lookout for kids who don't have shoes, so I can get them some.
Magazine Street, 1983

Chapter 11

Katrina: Lest We Forget

Weather Forecast

"It's going to Apalachicola late Sunday as a Category 2 storm."
Channel 6, 5:00 P.M., Friday, August 26, 2005

Vortex of Doom

I realized Friday night that the rosy predictions on all the local stations were completely wrong. We were going to get hit, and hit hard. Having been through every Louisiana hurricane since 1947 and being totally prepared, I opted to stay put and not risk being trapped on an interstate with my faithful dogs. After nailing up the last boards, I went out to the Mandeville lakefront and saw this image of impending doom.
Mandeville lakefront facing southeast, August 28, 2005

Pittman v. Corps of Engineers, 1992

To understand why the levees collapsed (none of the major breaks was caused by "overtopping"), one has to understand that ordinary citizens trusted the Levee Board and the U.S. Army Corps of Engineers. Few knew that the levees were "upgraded" in the early 1990s with silt from the Mississippi River-Gulf Outlet dredging and not with clay mud that could stop water. In 1985, the Corps conducted tests in the Atchafalaya Basin using the same materials and design of the "upgrades" being made along the major canals in New Orleans. At exactly eight feet of water, the test levees collapsed, but for "economic reasons" the Corps ordered Pittman Brothers Construction to proceed "as is." Pittman filed suit in federal court and lost, so the die was cast. The levees were not safe, and the Corps knew it twenty years before the disaster in 2005. I was out there at those levees testing a 4x5 view camera during the construction and I was not aware that those sheet piles were not being driven deep enough to hit clay. This is why we say correctly that the flood was "manmade."
Seventeenth Street Canal, Jefferson Parish side, 1993

"Katrina Takes Aim"

Newspaper found on the steps of an office a week after the floodwaters had receded.
Canal Street, 2005

"R.I.P. Fats"

There was great sorrow for all New Orleanians when it was announced that Fats Domino had perished in the flood. Apparently, FEMA did not know that Antoine Domino was in fact the Fats Domino, who was safe in a shelter in Baton Rouge.
Fat's house in the Ninth Ward, 1200 block of Caffin Avenue, 2005

Mike's Hardware

Mike LaFleur is a retired NOPD officer. When he's not pursuing his career as bass drummer for the Gentilly Brass Band, he operates Mike's Hardware on Elysian Fields. He comes from a Marine family and is damn proud of it.
Elysian Fields near Gentilly Boulevard, 2005

Where Is FEMA?

This was the question on everyone's mind from the moment the winds died down. For days we had no assistance from FEMA, and that created the disaster on top of the disaster called Katrina.
Lakeview house, 2006

Roots

Lower Ninth Ward house with ancient oak pulled from the ground.
St. Claude below the Industrial Canal, 2005

We Are . . . New Orleans!

Uncle Jerry's shirt says it all on Mardi Gras Day 2006. Those of us who stayed lived in a ghost town for years. That first Halloween and Mardi Gras were like one of those science-fiction movies from the '50s when all the people were gone. The Stompers, Tumblers, and Gentilly Brass Band combined to barely make up a full band that played to empty streets.
Decatur Street, 2006

Bent but Not *Broken*

The neutral ground on St. Charles Avenue looked like ground zero. Streetcars would not roll there for a very long time.
St. Charles Avenue upriver of Audubon Park, 2005

Last Message

A day before Katrina hit, the owners of a nursing home in St. Bernard were offered two school buses to evacuate under a mandatory order from the parish. For reasons that remain controversial, they refused the offer, and thirty-five patients perished in a ten-foot surge and flood that came the next night. Someone had placed this message for their relatives beneath the clock in the hall, approximately nine feet above the floor.
St. Bernard Parish, 2005

Funeral for a Veteran

As the victims of the flood were slowly identified, the funerals began. Young Men Olympian and Young Tuxedo gave one of the brothers a proper jazz funeral. This was the first jazz funeral after Katrina in Central City.
2005

"Cross Over the Bridge"

In an incident immediately after Katrina, flood victims were told to cross the Crescent City Connection in order to find shelters and transportation on the Westbank. After walking from the Superdome across the bridge, they were met by law enforcement, who refused to let them proceed. Some reports said shots were fired over the heads of the victims of the flood. In a funeral for the first three deceased to be buried, it was decided to start in Gretna, not far from where the incident had occurred. Eleven Young Tuxedo members were flown in from all over the U.S. where they had evacuated to, and the funeral ended at the gazebo next to Woldenberg Park. These were the only eleven musicians in the entire city of New Orleans that day.
Woldenberg Park, 2005

Coast Guard Station

Katrina's winds and waves were too much for this New Orleans landmark, the Coast Guard Station at West End. Happily, it stands today, restored, on its original site.
Lakeshore Drive, 2006

We Survived

Sign on a Gentilly house.
Franklin Avenue, 2006

Deano and Grayce Assunto

Standing proudly in front of their flood-damaged house, the Assuntos display their American flag, Original Dukes of Dixieland poster, and determination to return home and rebuild their lives. Deano is the son of Frank Assunto, the leader of the Original Dukes of Dixieland, which became one of the greatest jazz bands in the world. When it came time to decide on where to watch the Saints in the Super Bowl, there was only one place to be! Jan (Freddie and Betty Assunto's daughter) had her voodoo dolls, and I brought the "Who Dat" champagne for what was a most memorable night.
Metry, 2006

"Only being fifteen years old when my dad, Frank Assunto, died, it took me years to collect photos, recordings, and videos of my family's musical legacy, which dates back to 1925 with Papa Jac Assunto and his two sons, Freddie and Frank, who founded the Dukes of Dixieland in 1950-51. When my wife, Grayce, and I saw the size of Hurricane Katrina and it was headed our way, it only took a second for us to decide to evacuate, as we had done for smaller storms in the past. Prior to Katrina we would evacuate and return with no problem. People would ask me why do I do this each time, and my reply was always the same. 'One day we'll leave and we won't be able to return, and if that happens I'll have with me what's most important.' Sadly that came true with Katrina as many folks lost everything and couldn't return home.

I feel fortunate, even though our home was flooded and we lost everything under the four-foot mark. We had evacuated to Bentonville, Arkansas with all those Assunto/Dukes items, which also included my dad's trumpets.

I feel we beat Katrina hands down by coming home and rebuilding our home and preserving the Assunto legacy so it can be shared for years to come."

—Deano Assunto

New Orleans, Proud to Call It Home

The day after the winds ceased, I instinctively collected shower curtains and nails to start patching roofs, as was my family's tradition. The Richardson Roofing and Sheet Metal company was founded in 1912. My grandfather taught me that when a disaster struck, we would go out with rolls of tar paper and nails and patch the roofs of our customers. We left a note on the house if no one was there that said, "This repair is free. If it leaks, let us know. When we have time, we will come fix it properly at normal rates." That was the foundation of what became known as the Arabi Wrecking Krewe. After Katrina, I did my first repairs on neighbors' houses on September 2, 2005, in Mandeville and Lacombe. I got to New Orleans as quickly as possible, three days after the flood.
Arabi, 2005

6026

This was my first house, on St. Anthony Avenue. It was flooded in 1995 and I reluctantly decided to move to "higher ground" in Mandeville. After losing everything three times in floods, I realized that I was going to have to relocate to protect my photographs and negative files. The water at my old house after Katrina was 11.5 feet, and it stayed for many weeks and had to be pumped out. The house is still there and I wish I could have stayed, but I knew that those levees were substandard and would one day collapse. See my "Pittman v. Corps of Engineers" photo to find out what I knew years before the manmade flood of 2005.
Gentilly, 2005

Venezia

This New Orleans mainstay since 1957 was flooded just like the rest of Mid-City. It is restored and open today, just down the street from Brocato's Ice Cream.
North Carrollton Avenue, 2006

"Brian's Song"

Brian O'Neill was a well-known, respected, and loved musician who exemplified professionalism and character. Like all of us, he was severely impacted by what had happened to New Orleans and it may have played a part in his untimely death. All of the musicians who were in New Orleans turned out for his jazz funeral. Deacon John sang "Many Rivers to Cross," and the band marched up and down an almost deserted St. Charles Avenue. Wesley Schmidt led the procession, and the sound reverberating off those distant walls was a fitting tribute to Brian.
St. Charles Avenue at Louisiana Avenue, 2005

Ben Smith

A huge tree fell on Ben Smith's Lacombe residence in the storm. The very first "wrecking krewe" I formed six days after Katrina went over there with just five people to see if we could put tarps on the roof and do something with the tree. Ben was up on a ladder, stapling the plastic over a hole in the roof, when the ladder collapsed and Ben fell and broke his left wrist. He waited eleven hours to see an orthopedic surgeon, who put on a cast and said he would have to wait days for surgery. While Ben headed to Florida to get surgery, we continued patching the roof and returned later with a chainsaw to try to cut away the trees. It took four hours to cut through the four-foot trunk of one of them. After a successful surgery, Ben had to play a gig in Las Vegas, holding the horn with severe pain. Ben's wrist is OK now, but it was quite an ordeal before he got medical attention and recovered fully. Like so many others, Ben joined with the Arabi Wrecking Krewe as a board member and also played for benefits such as the "Pay the Rent" event at Tipitina's.
Lacombe, 2005

Arabi Wrecking Krewe

The group started out with me and four volunteers on September 4, 2005, just a few people helping others with worse damage to their homes. It rapidly grew into what became known as the Arabi Wrecking Krewe after October of 2005. Ben Smith, Brenda Smith, Bill Phillips, and Bill's sister were the very first volunteers to join with me in salvaging Ben's home. Later, the name "Arabi Wrecking Krewe" was coined by Craig Kline (who had finally been able to return from Europe six weeks after the flood), when I took a gravel shovel and knocked down an entire wall with one hit in Arabi. Since we could see the Arabi water tower out the window, the comment was, "You are a one-man wrecking crew, the Arabi Wrecking Krewe." In time, the organization became a nonprofit and worked on 111 houses in three years.

Kidd Jordan's house, New Orleans East, 2007

Liberty Blues

As the Arabi Wrecking Krewe gained members and experience, we were able to move 100 cubic yards of debris out of a house in one day by hand. Specialists evolved. Someone would take out the moldings, others would remove the hot-water heater and appliances, others would tear out the sheetrock, and one group would try to salvage as many valuables as they could. Sometimes a "sculpture" would be built of some of the items recovered and left in front of the house as a sign that we had been there. A favorite pastime was "refrigerator throwing," where refrigerators were rolled out at high speed on a dolly and thrown on the trashpile. The record was awarded to Dr. Michael White for three complete flips of a full-sized model at his house on Chamberlain Drive. Mostly these activities were intended to break the tension of what was a grueling and heartbreaking task.
Chamberlain Drive, Gentilly, 2006

Melissa and Ward Reilly with their Favorite Son, "Fridge"

Antiwar activist, U.S. Army veteran, and "Veterans for Peace" member Ward and his wife, Melissa, are seen here in the French Quarter out on predawn "patrol." After Katrina, Ward organized several crews of Iraq and Vietnam veterans to help clear out damaged houses of other veterans in the New Orleans area. He worked tirelessly in the recovery effort, including directing supplies and donations to the Arabi Wrecking Krewe. This is 5:00 A.M. on Mardi Gras morning, on the way to try to find the Bone Men in Treme.
French Quarter, 2006

"I ended up in South Louisiana in 1963, after being transported here from the south side of Chicago when my parents divorced. My mom's parents had retired down here, and she needed some help because she had four children and no job, so to South Louisiana we came, and we never left. It was quite a culture shock, as you can imagine, but I fell in love with the creeks, bayous, and wildlife in Baton Rouge, immediately.

What brought me to New Orleans after Katrina was the fact that I'd been coming every week since early 2002 for antiwar organizing meetings, and many of my activist friends were affected by the disaster . . . plus, it was simply the right thing to do, of course. After months and months of relief work, I was a part of what I considered to be the best Mardi Gras ever. It was virtually only the locals who came out to that first New Orleans Mardi Gras after Katrina, basically, and simply, to see who all had survived. It was amazing."

—Ward Reilly

First Jazz Funeral After Katrina

Oswald Jones leads the "makeup" band through empty streets in Treme. It was quite a change from the thousands who marched with them before the storm.
Treme next to Armstrong Park, 2005

Oswald Jones

During the first jazz funeral after Katrina, the band was marching through Treme to empty streets. It was not the most encouraging situation, but when Oswald got that "Ghost in him," he jumped up on these steps, and the band filled those streets with the "fire of music" that either one "knows" or "never will."
Treme, 2005

Funeral for New Orleans

This captures the feeling we all had that day. To look around and only see seventy-five people at an event this significant, and then retire to empty streets and houses, was even more of a shock than the actual storm.
Woldenberg Park, 2005

Ray Nagin's Blues

I will always think that the shock of what happened not only took lives, it changed many forever. I never knew Mayor Ray Nagin personally, but I did not dislike him. Even now I think that what happened in those days, weeks, and months after the storm had a very negative impact on many.
Woldenberg Park, 2005.

Katrina Gras

The Society of St. Anne Marching Club procession on Mardi Gras morning from the Ninth Ward up to the Quarter had been a regular Storyville Stompers gig since 1979. After Katrina, by some miracle, the club put together the traditional march, only it started a block from Elysian Fields and the river instead of deep in the Ninth Ward. The colorful streamers signaled life rising out of the darkness of the flood.
Royal Street, 2006

What Parade?

On Mardi Gras Day, everyone is a parade, and often the official organized version is irrelevant. That's one of the secrets of being a New Orleanian: your entire life is a party; your entire career is fun. St. Anne always hits Canal in time for Rex to give his royal salute, as the band plays the "Triumphal March" from Aida. Bravo, Rex; bravo, Stompers!
French Quarter at Canal, 2006

Mike "the Lizard" Stuart

When employment opportunities were scarce, Mike moved to San Francisco to pursue his paralegal career. He was securely situated in California when Katrina hit. Since his mother still occupied his boyhood home, he returned several times, and we salvaged what we could of his magnificent silkscreens and his mother's treasures. When I told Mike that we were going to "march on Mardi Gras no matter what!" he instantly said, "I have to be there!" As a member of the Tumblers and Gentilly Brass Band, he would be a great addition to the band that day. The spirit of New Orleans knows no geographic boundaries. I have encountered it anywhere in the world I have been. The picture really says it all: "We shall return!"
French Quarter, 2006

"I was born in New Orleans and lived there for thirty-four years until my wife and I moved to Northern California in 1991. I met Sheik in the early 1980s while attending UNO, and he encouraged me to pick up and play my clarinet again when he formed the Gentilly Brass Band. When the 2006 Mardi Gras was coming around, Sheik encouraged me again to come back to New Orleans to march and play with the band in the French Quarter. Sheik and I both knew that it was going to be a very special Mardi Gras because this was going to show the rest of the country that New Orleans was truly recovered from the devastation of Hurricane Katrina.

Sheik took this photograph of me down in the Quarter just after sunrise on Mardi Gras morning. Besides playing with the band that day, my favorite time of coming back for this Mardi Gras was walking around the Quarter and the Faubourg Marigny early that morning and seeing and feeling the old city coming back to life and getting ready to have a great 'come-back-from-the-dead' party that Mardi Gras Day.

It was truly one of the best days of my life to be playing again with Sheik, Leroy Jones,Wesley Schmidt, and the rest of the gang of great New Orleans musicians. I, like Sheik, believe that the Mardi Gras of 2006 did prove to the world that New Orleans was truly back from the watery grave of Hurricane Katrina."

—Michael Stuart

"Ain't Daid Yet!"

That was the first thing Uncle Lionel said to me when he finally returned to New Orleans months after swimming out of his apartment using a bass drum as his flotation device. Dapper to the nines, Uncle was resplendent in his new suit, hat, cane, and, of course, his hand covered in diamonds. Yes, he even had "time on his hands" as always. Seeing Uncle that day, along with all the others who were straggling back as soon as they could, was when I think I knew that we were going to make it happen again.
Woldenberg Park, 2006

The Phoenix of New Orleans

At the first Jazz Fest after Katrina, the Arabi Wrecking Krewe was given ten passes for one day. At that time we only had ten regular members, so there was no problem with who got one. We decided that one day should be when the Stompers and Treme were playing on the Jazz Stage. When the Stompers came on, Wesley Schmidt, the "Prince of Gentilly," emerged in his resplendent lavender suit and lifted his symbolic "umbrella" to lead the second line. Again, the image demonstrates the determination and spirit that were going to revive New Orleans.
Jazz Fest, 2006

Don Vappie Pays the Rent

Everyone says that disaster brings out the best and the worst in people, and after going through so many disasters, I have to agree. Don Vappie was one of those who rose above to help others when he had lost so much himself. His "Pay the Rent" benefits not only raised money for those who desperately needed help but also served to inspire the volunteers who came from all over the world to help. Playing next to Don is Michael Doucet, founder of Beausoleil. Don is one of the greatest banjo, guitar, and bass players in the world, but you would never know it because of his kind, gentle, and humble disposition. He was a true hero of Katrina.
Howlin' Wolf, 2006

Lucien Barbarin

Grand-nephew of the great Paul Barbarin and one of the best entertainers from New Orleans, Lucien is famous for his incredible style and professionalism. He lost everything in Katrina, and yet he worked tirelessly to help raise money for others. Here he's playing at the "Pay the Rent" benefit sponsored by Don Vappie.
Howlin' Wolf, 2006

Hurricanes at Watson's House

The first offers of assistance after Katrina came from Europe, not from FEMA. Members of the Hurricane Brass Band from Maastricht, Netherlands contacted me the moment my phone was working again with donations to aid in the return of musicians to New Orleans. Here one of them, looking like a spaceman, is helping clear out Ernest Watson's Ninth Ward home. The saddest thing was how little we could salvage. Salt water and toxic chemicals in the floodwaters took a terrible toll.
Vicinity of Musicians' Village today, 2006

Hugo and Fats

Hugo Kuijpers, of the Hurricane Brass Band from Maastricht, was the stimulus for what I called, "Dedicated Funding," in which the donors would tell me where their money should go. I would then take a photograph of the recipient with their check, so everyone would know exactly where the money went. Dr. Klaus Lumma, a member of the Hurricanes, also contacted me with offers of assistance from Germany, and eventually he and Hugo became board members of the Arabi Wrecking Krewe as well. "Fats" started the St. Augustine/Arabi Wrecking Krewe Foundation in Germany and continues assisting the children of New Orleans with his Art Therapy Program in conjunction with Patrice Fisher and Carlos Valladares's Arpa group.
French Quarter Fest, 2008

"Why do I keep going to New Orleans? I've been loving to play New Orleans jazz since 1994 when I came for the first time. By then I played at Fritzel's. I was shocked to death in 2005 when my beloved Crescent City was hit so terribly— but soon after that I was blessed by many, many new friends: Sheik Richardson, Father LeDoux, Benny Jones, Patrice Fisher, Carlos Valladares, Edwin Gonzales, Ed Frieburg, Ben Smith, José Roberto Moreira, John Boutté, Leroy Jones, etc. They've all enriched my life and inspired my music. I am glad to be an external member of the St. Augustine Church, the Treme Brass Band, and Patrice Fisher's Arpa."

—Dr. Klaus Lumma

We Are NOPD

Nothing like Katrina had ever happened in New Orleans or even the United States before September of 2005. The NOPD had always responded to any hurricane by first making sure their families were safe and then going straight to their duty stations. Because of the "it's going to Florida" misinformation by weather commentators, we lost valuable days when we could have taken more steps to evacuate the city. So when the "mandatory evacuation orders" came out, there was chaos. We hear so much about police abandoning their duty, but few realize that all of the police cars, and very shortly all of the radios, became useless because of the nonexistent planning and execution by local emergency management, FEMA, and the state. So everyone was "on their own" almost immediately. The lack of any federal presence for six days did not help. It's very easy to criticize after the fact. But the fact is that the majority of NOPD did not abandon their jobs and did the best they could. Maj. Tim Bayard and reserve officers such as Lt. Joe Torregano led the effort to restore order and save lives, along with hundreds of other policemen. So I think it appropriate to remember those who did as well as those who did not.
Claiborne Avenue, circa 2008

Chapter 12

MONUMENTS

Awakening

I can remember exactly when I first became aware of something called "segregation." I was six or seven playing at Union Playground with some of the other kids in the neighborhood. We were playing touch football and having a grand time when a bike came up with two other kids on it. They asked if they could play and I said, "Sure." The game went on with one of the new kids on each team and we had a splendid time. The boy who joined our team must have been in the NFL later in life because every time he got the ball, he went all the way. After the game ended we all went home. My family was getting ready to listen to the radio, since no one had TVs yet. Our phone started ringing, and I could hear my parents speaking in serious tones that weren't normal. When my father came into my room, he asked what had happened at the playground that day. I told him we played football and that we had won the game. He went back to the constantly ringing phone and I could tell he was getting very angry. After a few more calls came in, he returned and said that I had "made a mistake" by playing in the game. In my very young mind I could not understand what he meant, because, as I kept telling him, we won the game. We heard a commotion out front and when we looked out the door, we saw a small fire on the lawn, behind the short hedges. My father ran out, put out the fire with the hose, and came back inside very angry. It seems that someone had put a two-foot-high cross made from sticks on our lawn and set it on fire. Later I would learn that those phone calls had been death threats against a six-year-old kid and the burning cross a sign that some very bad people did not like what I had done that afternoon. My father told me, "You did nothing wrong, but it's probably a good idea not to play with those kids again." That was my first experience with racism. I never understood it then, and I don't understand it now. I never saw those two little kids again but always wondered if they remembered our great afternoon of fun that day.

City Park, 2017

"Get in the Back of the Bus!"

It could not have been many more years later when my mother and I were going downtown on the public bus one early afternoon. I remember clearly that the bus was a very small one with the manufacturer's name, *White,* on the front. The sign above said *Franklin-Canal,* so I knew where we were going. In the front of every bus and streetcar, there are "beauty seats" that face the aisle. They are right behind the driver's seat and are still very popular with kids. So while my mother was paying the seven cents and getting a transfer for each of us, I jumped up on the "beauty seat" facing the driver's side of the bus. My mother sat down next to me, the only passengers on the bus. At the next stop, the bus halted and the doors opened. A lady with her little boy got on, and while his mother was paying the fares, he jumped up opposite me on the seat right behind the driver. He smiled and waved at me. I did the same. His mother sat down next to him, and the bus started forward. A few seconds later, the brakes slammed on and the bus suddenly stopped. The driver jumped up, stood over the lady and little boy, and started yelling at them, "Get in the back of the bus! You can't sit here." I was shocked and a little scared. The lady got up, but the little boy did not want to move. The driver became very angry and was yelling at the lady. She grabbed the little boy's arm and dragged him crying and screaming towards the back of the bus. The driver took a little wooden sign that was just one seat back from the beauty seats and brought it to the very last row. He put it into two little holes on the railings above the seat and told the lady to "get behind this sign or get off the bus." When he came charging back to the front of the bus, I looked up at him and said, "That's not nice." For what may have been the very first time, my mother slapped me in the face and said, "Be quiet." And so came my second realization about something I was later to learn was called "segregation."

Hayne Boulevard, 1988

Victory Barber Shop

Many years later I was in high school and going to church at least every Sunday and often early in the morning on school days. I would walk to St. James Major Church and knew everyone along the ten or so blocks I would go. High Mass was the really big deal at 11:00 A.M. on Sundays, and I went to it only very occasionally because it was much longer than a Low Mass. St. James Parish was upper middle class and almost every Mass was packed. There were seats along the walls for those who came after the regular pews were full. At one High Mass, I was on the right, about ten rows from the front. The priest was from Eastern Europe so he had an accent but everyone liked him. I can't remember his name, but I do remember the monsignor, Carl J. Shutten, who was in charge of the parish and whom we were all afraid of. I had never seen a Mass interrupted in my then fifteen-year-old life, but on this day Father Shutten came out of the sacristy with the purple ribbon around his neck indicating that he was "speaking for God" or something like that. He walked up to the podium while the Mass was in progress and said, *"Stop the Mass."* Everyone was shocked and total silence fell over the church. Even the priest at the altar had a very serious look on his face. Were the Russians attacking us? Did something terrible just happen? It did not take long to find out. "There's a nigger in my church!" Father Shutten almost yelled. "Where is the nigger?" he demanded, not once but three times. Everyone was in shock. Nothing like this had ever happened before and I think no one knew what to do or say. Then, over the dead silence of the congregation, this one lady stood up. I remember she had on a blue polka-dot dress and this really nice black hat. Next to her was a little boy who was also impeccably dressed. When she stood, Father Shutten said, "Get out of *my* church, nigger, and don't come back." As she tearfully and silently started to walk out of the church, I got up and went out the side door. All eyes were on her so I don't think anyone saw me leave. That was my last High Mass and an event etched in my mind forever. I know that at that moment I lost all respect for Father Shutten and never wanted to see him again. The seeds of religious doubt had been planted in me, because he was wearing that purple ribbon that supposedly meant he was "speaking for God." From then on it was only God in my mind, not anyone speaking for God.
Central City, 1972

At the Foot of Canal Street

It was 1968 and I was now questioning everything. My time in the Marines and Navy gave me insight into what war really was, not what was portrayed in the movies. When I read an *Esquire* magazine on the front porch of our house at 3607 Clermont Drive in April of 1968 and learned that the "accepted" story about the Gulf of Tonkin Incident was possibly false, my future "forensic investigator" career began. So one day when I was on the way to the Canal Street ferry, I got off the Canal streetcar and decided to look behind the tall hedges right at the end of the line. I was surprised to see a very tall monument all but hidden by the shrubs. I went up to read what it said. Words such as *The Good White People, Usurpers,* and *White Supremacy* were written on it. I was shocked to see those things so prominently displayed on what was called "The Liberty Monument." I told someone I knew about it. He went out there and was surprised to find the same things I had. We agreed that statue had to come down. Little did we know it would take almost fifty years for that to happen.
Foot of Canal Street, 1971

It's My Heritage

As I read the names of those who had been involved in the rebellion of 1874 that the Liberty Monument commemorated, I was surprised to find Lt. F. L. Richardson listed. While I have not yet had time to fully research any direct connection, that name, *Richardson,* was on that monument. So part of my heritage is at least indirectly linked to what that monument actually commemorated, white supremacy. I have always opposed such an idea and surely do now.
Foot of Canal Street, 1971

Black Power

As public awareness grew about the existence of this monument that had been hidden away from casual view by the huge bushes that had been planted around it, it started receiving paint spatters, spray-painted graffiti, and sledgehammer blows. Finally it was moved to a less conspicuous location on Iberville Street. Controversy continued to stalk it, leading to today's Take 'Em Down NOLA movement.
Foot of Canal Street, 1968

"Racism, controversy, and the Big Easy. Some call this vandalism and some call it righting a wrong. Urban legend or truth: in the small hours of a cold rainy morning, two men on a motorcycle rode past the statue that was once at the foot of Canal Street and splashed indelible black ink on it, setting the stage for more attacks and the eventual removal of the statue."

—Jerry Steubben, New Orleans native, playwright, and drug counselor

Moon Walk

When Maurice "Moon" Landrieu ran for mayor, I was working at WYLD Radio. I met him while he was standing in the street at Galvez and Canal, walking up to cars, shaking hands, and asking for support. I was very impressed that this well-known and successful city councilman would take the time to be out campaigning in inclement weather. Moon seemed like a "regular guy" who actually cared about the city and its people, rather than his own power and personal advancement. We gave him our votes, and when he was inaugurated in 1970, I went to Duncan Plaza to hear what he had to say. A portion of that speech is now emblazoned on a plaque at the Moon Walk, along the river across from Jackson Square. His words impressed me enough that I sought out employment at City Hall and wound up working under his administration in the Food Stamp and Model Cities programs. On several occasions I had personal dealings with him, notably the weekend after the Howard Johnson sniper incident, when he was in Audubon Park with his huge Great Dane that chased after my Siberian puppy. We chased the big dog down and nothing happened to the little puppy. Only as the gentleman was apologizing profusely did I realize it was the mayor, without bodyguards and just enjoying the cold winter's morning out in the park. Moon had style, courage, integrity, grace, and class. These comments from his inaugural address speak volumes about one of our best mayors ever: "Let us be guided then by a sense of justice. Let us build a system of just laws and demand adherence to those laws. Let us create a city of equal opportunity for all, with all sharing in both the responsibilities and benefits. Let us create a city where neither the choice of religion nor the accident of color is an obstacle to opportunity and advancement, nor a substitute for effort and ability."

Moon Walk, 2005

Facing North

Until now, there never was a time after 1884 that the statue of Robert E. Lee was not standing high above the spot that came to be known as "Lee Circle." It took over one hundred years, but a national movement to take down all the artifacts that honor the Confederate "Lost Cause" has emerged. Much controversy ensued, but in the end, the "Nuremberg" solution has prevailed. When the U.S. reached Berlin in 1945, all the Nazi statues and buildings were blown up. When the U.S. reached Baghdad in 2003, the first thing the citizenry did was topple the Saddam Hussein statue. Everyone will have their own perspective on this, and that is their right. In my view, based upon my family history, I want all the Confederate monuments taken down and put into museums, just as the German people did with the Nazi artifacts.
Lee Circle, 2017

"A Change Is Gonna Come"

It has been many decades since I witnessed members of the NOPD dragging the Reverend A. L. Davis from the cafeteria in City Hall. His head bounced off the granite steps as he was arrested and taken to jail. During that same timeframe, peaceful "sit-in" protesters were beaten by segregationists, arrested, and also taken to jail. It's only been a few decades since blacks and whites could sit together on the bus or at Saints games to cheer on our team. It has been my experience that many of those who support the "heritage" of the Confederate statues have never felt the sting of discrimination or the denial of their constitutionally guaranteed rights. My father did not teach me to hate; my mother dedicated her life as a Red Cross nurse to helping anyone in need. My longtime friend Deputy Chief Charles Ladell of the NOPD always told me, "I was promoted because I was not a racist." Whenever I am confronted with racism, I say, "Close your eyes and tell me what color I am."
St. Charles Avenue looking west, 2017

Who's It Gonna Be?

Now that the Confederate monuments are gone, what is going to replace them? In a city like New Orleans, there is no shortage of likely replacements. How about honoring Louis Armstrong, Pete Fountain, Louis Prima, or George Lewis? There are literally hundreds of New Orleanians who deserve being honored. Henry Dudley, Hap Glaudi, Dooky Chase, Nick Castrogiovanni, Al Hirt, Mahalia Jackson, Fats Houston, Tuba Fats, Mel Leavitt, Joe Gemelli, Nash Roberts, Mel Parnell, Frank Assunto, Papa Celestin, Fats Domino, Dr. Norman C. Francis, Andrew Higgins, Chep Morrison, Allen Toussaint, Dr. John, Terry Duvernay, Mr. Bingle, Buster Holmes, Chief William McCrossen NOFD, the Sterns, Lelia Haller . . . it's a very, very long list of "possibles." We could even have rotating statues and a park somewhere where all the new monuments could be placed. Let's honor those who created and made the world better, not those who destroyed and killed.
City Park main entrance, 2017